STEP-BY-STEP

50 Recipes for Kids to Cook

STEP-BY-STEP
50 Recipes for Kids to Cook

Judy Williams

Photography by David Jordan

LORENZ BOOKS
LONDON • NEW YORK • SYDNEY • BATH

For John and Chloe: years apart
but chips off the same block.

First published in 1996 by Lorenz Books

© 1996 Anness Publishing Limited

Lorenz Books is an imprint of
Anness Publishing Limited
Boundary Row Studios
1 Boundary Row
London SE1 8HP

ISBN 1 85967 135 7
A CIP catalogue record is available from the British Library

Publisher: Joanna Lorenz
Senior Cookery Editor: Linda Fraser
Junior Editor: Emma Brown
Designer: Lilian Lindblom
Food and props styling for photography: Judy Williams
Assistant Home Economist: Manisha Kanani

Printed and bound in Hong Kong

For all recipes, quantities are given in both metric and imperial measures, and
where appropriate, measures are also given in standard cups and spoons. Follow one set,
but not a mixture, because they are not interchangeable.

CONTENTS

INTRODUCTION

Welcome to the wonderful world of food. We all need it, we all eat it and now you're going to find out how to cook it.

It would be easy never to prepare a meal again – supermarkets are choc-a-bloc with ready-made meals, but where's the fun in that? It's true you'll have to find time to shop and get everything ready, as well as doing the actual cooking, but the thrill of serving and eating something you have made with your own clean hands is fantastic.

This book is split into sections. The first part is the bossy bit, which tells you what to do and what not to do to be safe in the kitchen.
Then there's lots of information about equipment and about words used in cooking that you might not understand. After that it's on to the exciting bit – choosing what to cook. Some recipes are simple and these are a good place to start, if you haven't done any cooking before. There are also lots of recipes that seem more difficult but, in fact, just take a bit longer.

All basic cooking techniques have been included in one recipe or another, so you will learn lots of useful skills that can be swapped around as you get more experienced. These skills may be useful for some school exams, and will certainly be invaluable when you leave home and have to feed yourself. You'll probably be feeding your friends as well, once they learn of your talents!

As well as stacks of snacks and savoury meals, there are plenty of puddings, cakes and biscuits to choose from, with chocolate included in as many as possible!

So get cooking and have a great time!

Getting Switched On

The kitchen is full of things that could be very dangerous, such as electrical sockets, hot ovens and hobs, fast-moving equipment and hot pans and baking tins. It's therefore very important that you take as much care as possible.

Tie long hair back while you are cooking – then it can't get caught on equipment, will keep away from flames and won't become an extra ingredient in your recipe!

Always wash your hands – not just when you begin to cook but as you handle different ingredients. Garlic-flavoured cakes are disgusting and no one finds grey pastry attractive!

Water and electricity don't mix, so dry your hands before touching any sockets or plugging in machinery. Switch off before pulling out the plug.

Read through the recipe before you start. Have everything ready: panic causes problems! Protect your clothes: wear an apron or old shirt if you are a messy cook, and roll up those sleeves!

Washing up is the most boring part about cooking, so keep it to a minimum and wash up as much as possible as you go along. Or stack the dishwasher, of course, but in all events, try to leave the room tidy or your days in the kitchen may be numbered!

Is the work surface too high? Making pastry or cakes means working in a mixing bowl and it might be hard to get your hands right in there. Put the bowl on the kitchen table or stand it in the empty sink instead, as both these places are much lower than a kitchen work surface.

Too hot to handle? Always use oven gloves or a thickly folded, dry tea towel (wet ones let the heat straight through) to lift things in and out of the oven. Keep saucepan handles turned away from any heat source and check they aren't hot, before trying to lift the pan.

Water, water everywhere: some recipes call for hot liquids and foods to be drained or poured into something else. Please do this very carefully.

Don't overfill the pan and, if it's too heavy or you aren't sure you can manage, ask a grown-up for some help.

A helping hand? Watch out for younger members of the family who want to help, especially if the oven is hot or you are frying things. If they really won't go away, find them something simple to do, such as arranging tomatoes in a bowl, or greasing cake tins; give them a small piece of pastry or dough to play with. Pets can also be a hazard: they creep in and try to trip you up, so bear them in mind.

Whoops-a-daisy: any wet spills on the floor, especially oil, should be wiped up at once. Use hot, soapy water and then rub the area dry so the floor doesn't become a skating rink.

All this is not really complicated: it's a matter of being careful and sensible and thinking about what you are doing. Remember that most accidents happen in the home: make sure you aren't one of them!

Equipment

All cooking jobs in the kitchen need a tool of some sort, although a few basic ones can do most jobs. The biggest one is the cooker.

Cookers

There are lots of different types but you are sure to have one, if not two, of the more popular ones. They are made to work using different sorts of energy and each one has its own temperature guide, which explains why recipes have a choice of three settings for preheating the oven, for example, "Cook at 200°C/400°F/Gas 6". If you have an electric cooker that works at Centigrade temperature (°C), use the first number. For an electric cooker that uses Fahrenheit (°F), use the second number and for a gas cooker use the last number.

The oven is hottest on the top shelf, although most things are best cooked on the middle one. If two baking trays are going in at the same time, the one nearer the top of the oven will be cooked more quickly.

When the recipe says to preheat the oven, remember it will take about 10 minutes to reach the specified temperature; if you put the food in before the oven is hot enough, it will take longer to cook and some food will not cook correctly.

Cookers usually have three different cooking places – the oven, the grill and the hob.

The oven cooks large items of food slowly and evenly, with the minimum of attention.

The grill cooks quickly, so grilled food must be smaller and thinner or the outside will burn before the middle is properly cooked (even though there is a temperature control). You have to keep a close watch on the food and it will need to be turned often.

The hob is the name for the four burners or hot plates on the top of the oven: in some kitchens, the hob is separate from the oven. You use saucepans or frying pans to cook food on the hob. Control-knobs can be turned up to cook things more quickly, or turned down low to cook more slowly.

Timers

Modern cookers often have a built-in timer, rather like an alarm clock. Set it to the recommended cooking time and it makes a horrible buzzing noise that reminds you to take the food out.

Microwave Ovens

These machines make all the water molecules in food jump around and heat up, which cooks food quickly. They are brilliant at thawing frozen food, re-heating cooked food, melting chocolate and cooking jacket potatoes. But most of them can't turn food brown or cook large amounts of anything.

Safety First for Microwave Ovens

Never put any foil, metal dishes or plates with metallic edges in microwaves, and follow recipe instructions carefully.

The standing time mentioned at the end of lots of microwave recipes is part of the cooking, so don't be tempted to skip it.

Safety First for Ovens and Hobs

When the oven is working, obviously the door becomes very hot and this can be dangerous if you have younger brothers and sisters who want to help. If your cooker is new it may have a stay-cool door, which is much safer. Otherwise, watch out for this.

Green Tips for Ovens and Hobs

Save energy and cut fuel bills:
- Only use as much water as you need in pans and kettles.
- Put lids on saucepans and reduce the heat once the contents have come to the boil.
- Flames that lick up the sides of a pan are wasting energy, so adjust the flame.
- Steam a second vegetable in a colander over the potatoes.
- Try to cook more than one thing in the oven at a time.

Working Tools

There are probably lots of weird and wonderful things in the kitchen cupboards and drawers, here's a guide to help you find out what they do.

Food Processor

This is actually a giant blender, with a large bowl and, usually, lots of attachments. The metal chopping blade is the one we use most, it's best with dry ingredients like vegetables and pastry. The plastic blade is for batters and cakes. Some processors also have grating blades and slicing plates.

Electric Whisk

A whisk's main function is to beat in air and make the mixture bigger and thicker, as in, for example, cream and cake mixtures. But a whisk can also blend things together and make them smooth, such as sauces.

Blenders

Also called liquidizers, these are usually attached to an electric whisk motor or a food processor and are tall and deep, with blades at the base. Ideal for turning things into liquid such as fruit for sauces, soups and milk shakes. Hand-held blenders are much smaller and can be used in a small bowl or mug.

Safety First for Whisks, Blenders and Processors

Never put your hand in the processor to move something while it is plugged in. And keep small fingers away from whisks while they are whizzing round.

Treat all electrical equipment very carefully and unplug everything before you fiddle around with blades.

Chopping Boards

Lots of people use the same board for all their preparation, but it's much more hygenic to use a different one for each type of job. It is possible to buy boards with coloured handles, so the same one is always used for the same job. A wooden board is best for cutting bread. Scrub boards well after use.

Graters

A pyramid-shaped or box-shaped grater is the most useful type. Each side has a different grating surface, made up of small, curved, raised blades. Use the coarsest one for vegetables and cheese and the finer sides for grating orange and lemon rind. Stand grater on a flat surface while you use it and grated food collects inside the pyramid. Scrub well with a brush after use. There are also very small graters, for whole nutmegs.

Measuring Equipment

Most homes have some sort of measuring equipment, whether this is scales, spoons or cups.

Recipes seem to have lots of weights listed; this is because different countries use different ways to measure things. As long as you stick to the same ones for each recipe, you shouldn't have any problems.

The metric quantity is mentioned first, such as 115 g, followed by the old imperial measurement – 4 oz – and these are ways to measure dry ingredients, such as flour, vegetables and chocolate (most important!).

When you measure liquids, there are three measurements to choose from. The metric measurement, such as 300 ml, followed by ½ pint – the imperial one; and, finally, 1¼ cups, which is the American measure. Most measuring jugs have all these measurements written on the side for easy measuring.

Small amounts of both dry and wet ingredients are often measured in millilitres (ml) and tablespoons (tbsp). 15 ml is the same as 1 tbsp and 5 ml is the same as 1 teaspoon (1 tsp). The spoon should be level.

Bowls

Mixing bowls come in all sorts of sizes and the most useful are made from heatproof glass. Use large ones for pastry, bread-making and whisking egg whites; smaller ones are better for smaller quantities, such as beating eggs and mixing dips.

Pans

Saucepans and frying pans can be made from different metals; some are even glass! The most popular are aluminium pans and stainless steel ones. Pans need to have a thick base to stop food from sticking.

colander

nutmeg grater

baking tray

bun tin

saucepans

saucepan

springform cake tins

frying pan

wire cooling rack

grater

muffin tin

whisks

measuring cups

weighing scales

food processor

mixing bowls

electric blender

measuring spoons

chopping boards

measuring jug

Small Tools

Can opener
The two "arms" are squeezed together, so the blades at the top pierce the can. Turn the handle round and round and the top of the can will come off.

Canelle knife
This is rather like a zester, but cuts a thicker strip of rind.

Corer
Looks rather like a potato peeler but has a tube of metal that is pushed through the centre of an apple to pull out the core.

Fish/egg slice
For lifting and turning burgers, fish, or even eggs!

Garlic press
Squashes the garlic cloves through small holes ready for cooking; you need a brush with stiff bristles to poke through the holes to get it clean again.

Hand whisk
A spring whisk is most effective, good for cream or eggs.

Kitchen scissors
Used for cutting things like bacon, but also perfect for snipping herbs.

Knives
I am sure you know that knives must be used very carefully, but it's easy to get careless. Don't use a huge bread knife to peel an apple: pick the right size for the right job and try not to be distracted. No conducting with the carving knife!

You will only need five basic knives to do most jobs in this book. *Paring knife*, with an 8cm/3in blade, for peeling and trimming fruit and vegetables. *Cook's knife*, with a 15cm/6in blade, for general slicing. *Chopping knife*, with a 20cm/8in blade, for chopping and slicing. *Bread knife*, with a 25cm/10in serrated-edge blade, for cutting bread. *Palette knife,* with a long, flexible blade, for lifting and spreading. All knives get blunt after a while and should be sharpened carefully, using a special knife-sharpening gadget.

Ladle
A large, deep spoon, used mainly for serving soup.

Lemon squeezer
The cut side of a halved citrus fruit is pressed down and squeezed over the central "spike". The juice runs down and collects, ready for pouring.

Pastry brush
For brushing egg on to pastry; also good for brushing sauces or oil over meat or vegetables.

Pastry wheel
Used for making a decoratively cut edge for pastry or ravioli.

Piping bag and nozzles
Big ones are best for biscuit mixes. A nozzle is dropped into the bag until it peeps out of the other end. Small ones are better for piping icing.

Potato peeler
Some have fixed peeler blades with wooden handles; others have a more mobile blade and this can make peeling easier.

Rolling pin
Usually wooden, although marble ones keep pastry cool.

Rubber spatula
A wooden handle with a flexible blade, it's very good at getting mixing bowls clean.

Sieves
These come in various sizes. A small one is ideal for sifting icing sugar over cakes. Larger ones are used for sifting flour and draining vegetables.

Skewers
Metal or wooden ones are used for kebabs; metal ones are also good for pushing into cakes, to see if they're cooked.

Slotted spoon
For lifting and draining food.

Tongs
Used for turning things over.

Wooden spoons
Come in various lengths. Short ones are better for beating cake mixtures and chocolate, but ones with longer handles are better for cooking on the hob, because your hand is further from the heat.

Zester
A small tool with five tiny round blades at the end. When it is dragged across an orange or lemon, it removes long thin shreds of rind that can be used in a recipe or as a garnish.

lemon

hand whisk

piping bag and

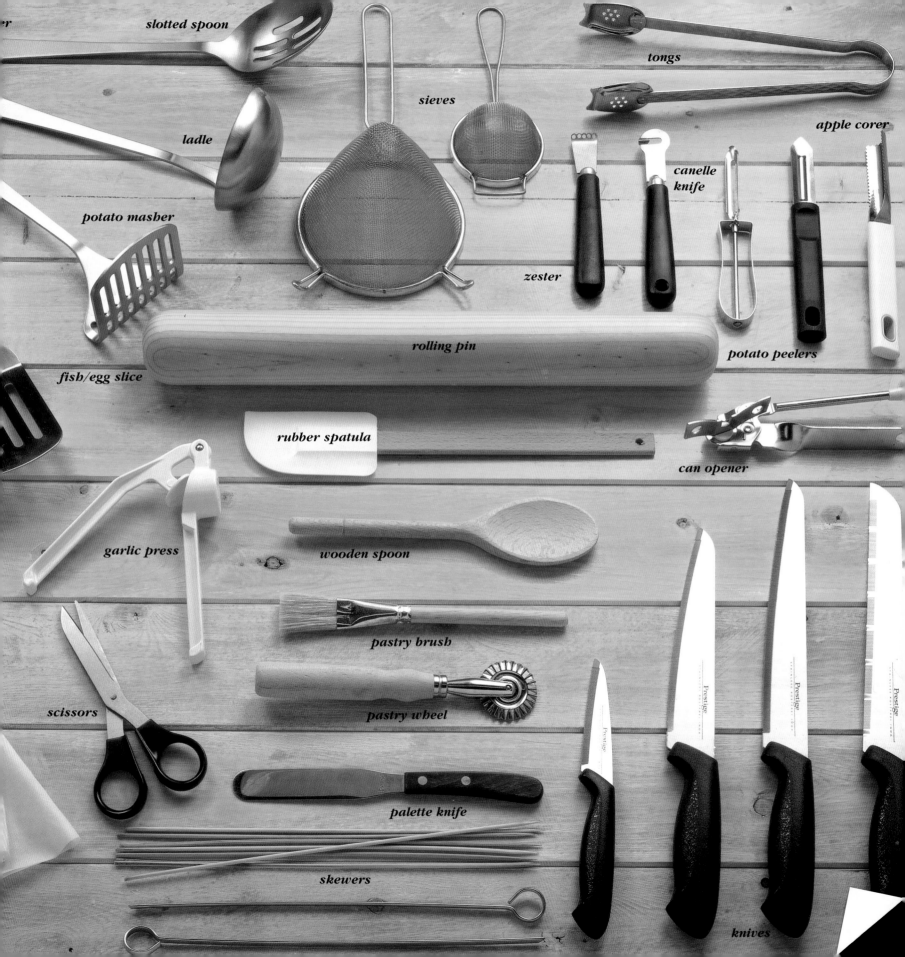

slotted spoon

tongs

sieves

ladle

apple corer

canelle knife

potato masher

zester

rolling pin

potato peelers

fish/egg slice

rubber spatula

can opener

garlic press

wooden spoon

scissors

pastry brush

pastry wheel

palette knife

skewers

knives

A–Z of Cooking Terms

Sometimes cookery seems like a foreign language, with lots of words you aren't sure about. Hopefully this A–Z guide will explain what most of them mean and then you will be off your marks and in action in the kitchen.

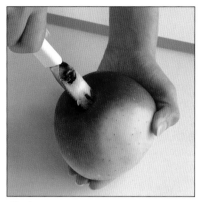

Coring

Dredging

Bake
To cook in the oven, in dry heat, at a set temperature.

Barbecue
A method of cooking food over glowing charcoal, which gives food a smoky taste.

Baste
To spoon fat and cooking juices over meat whilst cooking, to keep the meat tender and moist.

Blend
To mix ingredients evenly. Also used to describe the action of a blender.

Boil
A liquid is boiling when the edges are rolling over and large bubbles are heaving in the surface. This is called a rolling boil and that's how it looks. Usually, at this point, the heat is turned down and the liquid starts to simmer. There aren't many things that are cooked at a rolling boil, except raw beans, pasta, and caramel. The action would be too fierce for most vegetables.

Bone
To remove bones from meat, fish or poultry.

Brown
Meat and vegetables are often browned at the start of a recipe, to give a good, even colour and a more savoury flavour. The food is turned over frequently, usually in hot fat.

Core
To cut out the tough central part and seeds of a fruit. This is easiest done with a corer. Push it into the apple, over the stalk, and twist. Pull the corer out and the core will come out as well.

Cream
To beat fat (usually butter or magarine) and sugar together until they are light and fluffy, when making cakes.

Dredge
To cover something with an even layer of flour or sugar, dredging chocolate brownies with icing sugar for instance.

Dust
To sprinkle food lightly with flour or sugar – like dusting a loaf with flour before baking.

Flake
To divide cooked fish into its natural flakes having removed any skin and bones.

Fold in
To add something to a mixture very gently, so as not to break up all the air bubbles – as when folding whisked egg white into soufflés, and flour into sponge cakes – so the mixture stays light and fluffy.

Fry
To cook food in hot fat or oil, usually to get a crisp, browned surface on the outside.

Garnish
To decorate savoury food with herbs, chopped vegetables or fruit, to make it look attractive before serving.

Glaze
Brushing pastry or bread with egg or milk will make it shiny and look more attractive.

Grate
To shred into tiny strips using a grater. (See also page 18).

Grease
Brushing cooking tins or trays with a little oil or a margarine wrapper helps to prevent food from sticking while it cooks.

Knead
To work dough until it is smooth and elastic (stretchy).

Line a tin
Putting a paper lining inside the tin, to prevent food sticking.

Marinade
A flavoured liquid, usually savoury and using oil, lemon juice or wine. Meat is sometimes soaked in a marinade to make it more tender and tasty.

Marinate
To leave meat, fish or poultry in a marinade for a while.

Par-boil
To start cooking food, like potatoes, in boiling water, before moving on to the next stage of the cooking process, such as roasting. Par-boiling speeds up the roasting time.

Pipe
To force food from a piping bag through a plain or star nozzle into decorative shapes. Large nozzles might be used for biscuits, cream or mashed potato and smaller ones for icing.

Folding in

Garnishing

Rubbing in

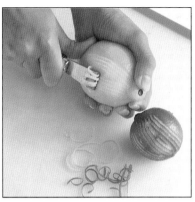

Zesting

Poach
To cook food gently in simmering, not boiling, water.

Prove
Once bread dough has been kneaded for 5 minutes and is smooth and elastic, it is covered and left somewhere warm to double in size. This is called proving the dough.

Purée
To turn soft, solid food into a smoother thicker food – for example, lumpy vegetable soup can be puréed in a blender to make it smooth.

Roast
To cook uncovered in the oven by dry heat.

Roux
Equal quantities of butter or margarine and plain flour are cooked together, to make the thickening for a white sauce. The fat will be melted in a saucepan and then the flour mixed in. A roux should be cooked gently for 1–2 minutes before the liquid, usually milk, is added.

Rub in
To mix the fat into the flour when making pastry, crumble topping and some cakes. Use your fingertips to lift lumps of fat and flour and rub them together to break the fat into smaller and smaller pieces, until it looks like breadcrumbs. Hold your fingers high over the bowl to mix air into the mixture at the same time.

Seasoning
Seasoning usually means to add salt and pepper to savoury dishes, to heighten the flavour. Other aromatic ingredients added in small quantities, such as herbs, or chilli powder could also be called seasonings.

Shallow fry
To cook food in a thin layer of oil, so it browns and crisps on the outside.

Sieve
To shake dry foods through a sieve to remove any lumps. Also used to purée foods by pushing through the sieve, as an alternative to using a blender or food processor.

Simmer
To reduce the heat once the liquid has come to the boil so the liquid still bubbles lightly and is not completely calm.

Snipping
Using kitchen scissors to cut things in small pieces, rather than chopping them. A good way to cut up bacon, herbs, dried fruits and bread.

Stir-fry
A fast way to cook food over a high heat in very little oil. Food must be cut into small even-sized pieces and kept moving all the time to stop it burning. This is traditionally done in a wok, but a frying-pan can be used instead.

Stock
A tasty liquid that is used to make soups and cook rice. Vegetable trimmings and bones can be boiled in water and the water turns to stock as it picks up the flavour. It is quicker and easier to use stock cubes. They come in lots of flavours, so choose the one that suits your recipe best, for example, use chicken stock cubes for chicken dishes. Usually one stock cube is enough to flavour 600 ml/ 1 pint/2½ cups of water, but check the packet instructions.

Thicken
To give thinner sauces and gravies more body, by adding a thickening agent, such as cornflour. Mix it with a little water and pour it into the boiling liquid, stirring all the time (to stop it going lumpy), until it comes back to the boil and the liquid starts to thicken.

Whisk
To mix air into egg whites or yolks. Whisked egg whites go through several different stages as they thicken, so check the recipe carefully. "Soft peaks" means the egg white will stand in peaks but the tops will flop over. "Stiff peaks" means the peaks will not flop over; finally they become stiff and look dry.

Zest
To remove the coloured part of the rind of citrus fruit (lemons, oranges, etc.) use a fine grater or a zester. (See page 12).

TECHNIQUES

Preparing ingredients is easy when you follow
these step-by-step instructions.

Preparing Onions

Keeping the onions a similar size means they all
cook at the same time, but we don't want any
sliced fingertips, so take care!

Preparing Carrots

Although they are often just sliced in circles,
carrots can look much more attractive cut in a
different way.

1 Cut the onion in half with the skin
still on. Lie the cut side flat on a board.
Trim off both ends. Peel off the skin.

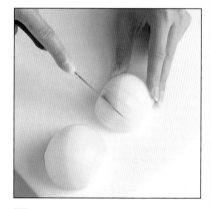

2 Make several parallel cuts lengthways (from trimmed end to end), but
not cutting right to one end.

1 Peel the carrot, using this quick method with a swivel peeler, and trim the ends.

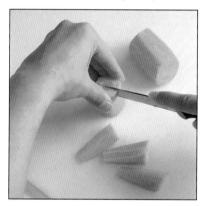

2 Cut the carrot into short lengths
and then into thin slices, lengthways.
You will need a sharp knife for this job,
so be careful.

3 Cut each thin slice into fine strips,
about the size of matchsticks.

3 Make cuts at right angles to the first
ones, at the same distance apart. The
onion will be finely chopped. Finally,
chop the end.

COOK'S TIP

When an onion is described as
"sliced", cut down through each
half to make vertical slices.

COOK'S TIP

Use tiny cutters to stamp out
shapes from the thin carrot slices,
to garnish soups or salads.

Grating Fresh Root Ginger

Ground ginger powder is fine in cakes, but when it comes to a stir-fry, it has to be fresh.

 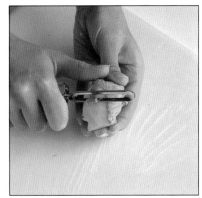

1 The size is often given as a measurement, because the root is long and knobbly and difficult to weigh accurately. Break off roughly the quantity you need.

2 Use a peeler, or sharp knife if the ginger is really lumpy, and cut away the tough outer layer.

3 Grate on the coarsest side of the grater and use the strips for your recipe. Don't use any hard or stringy bits of ginger.

COOK'S TIP
Fresh root ginger has a strong, spicy, flavour, so don't put in too much if you don't like hot food.

Grating Lemon Rind and Squeezing Lemon Juice

Recipes sometimes call for the grated rind and juice of a lemon.

1 Rinse the lemon, unless it was labelled "unwaxed". Rub the lemon up and down the fine grating side of the grater, until the yellow rind has come off. Stop grating once the white pith underneath shows through. Keep moving the lemon round the grater, until all the yellow rind is off.

 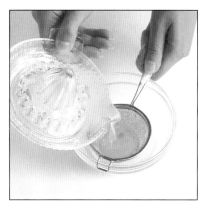

2 Cut the lemon in half, press one half down on to the pointed part of the squeezer and twist. Keep pressing and twisting and the juice will come out of the lemon. The larger pips all collect at the base and are held back by the glass "teeth".

3 Smaller pips might sneak through. Either fish them out with a spoon or your fingers, or pour the juice through a small sieve or tea strainer, before adding it to the mixture.

COOK'S TIP
Oranges and limes may be grated and squeezed the same way.

Separating Eggs

Meringues and some sauces call for just egg whites, so they must be separated from the yolk.

1 Break the egg on to a saucer.

2 Stand an egg cup over the yolk and hold it firmly in place, taking care not to puncture the yolk.

3 Hold the saucer over the mixing bowl and let the egg white slide in, hanging on to the egg cup. The yolk will be left on the saucer.

COOK'S TIP
The yolk may be needed for glazing, so check the recipe before you throw it away.

Grating

The most popular grater is the pyramid or box type, which offers different-sized blades for grating.

1 The very fine side is for grating whole nutmeg. Hold the nutmeg in one hand and rub it up and down the grater. Sometimes, it is easier to do this directly over the food.

2 The finer blades are best for citrus fruits. The blades only work downwards and you might need to brush out some of the rind from the inside with a dry pastry brush.

3 The coarsest side is best for cheese, fruit and vegetables. The blades work when you press downwards and the food will collect inside the grater.

COOK'S TIP
The jagged punched holes down one side of the grater are ideal for making breadcrumbs.

Whipping Cream

Cream can be bought in various thicknesses, so choose double, extra-thick or whipping cream, if you need it to be thick for your recipe. Don't try whipping single cream!

1 Pour the cream into a bowl and use an electric mixer to whip the cream. Keep the electric mixer moving around as you whisk.

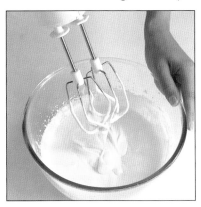

2 A hand-held whisk also works well but it takes much longer and makes your arm tired! The cream will first reach a soft and floppy stage, then get thicker and thicker the more you whisk.

3 Once whisk lines are left in the cream and it looks fairly stiff, it's time to stop whipping. Cream will start to look like mashed potato as it curdles and reaches the over-whipped stage.

Lining a Tin

Stop food, mainly cakes, sticking to the cooking tin by lining the tin with baking parchment or greaseproof paper.

1 Stand the tin on the paper and draw round the base. Cut out the shape, just inside the line.

2 Wrap a strip of paper round the outside of the tin and cut it 5 cm/2 in longer and 5 cm/½ in wider.

3 Fold one long edge over by 2.5 cm/1 in. Make diagonal cuts at regular intervals up to the fold. Grease the tin lightly, to help the paper stick to it. Put the long strip inside the tin, round the edges, so the fringed paper sits on the base. Lie the round piece of paper over the top.

COOK'S TIP

If you only need to base-line a tin, and not line the sides as well, just follow step 1.

Mix 'n' Match

Most dishes need something to go with them, to turn them into a complete meal.
Here are some quick easy ideas for accompaniments.

Making Mashed Potatoes

Check the labelling on the bags to see which potatoes are good for mashing, or ask your greengrocer.

Serves 4

INGREDIENTS
450 g/1 lb potatoes, peeled and
  quartered
25 g/1 oz/2 tbsp butter
30 ml/2 tbsp milk or cream
salt and pepper

1 Cook the potatoes in a pan with enough room to mash them. Cover with water, add a little salt and bring the water to the boil. Turn down the heat and simmer for 20–25 minutes. The potatoes should feel tender and fall off a sharp knife when cooked.

Cook's Tip
Add two crushed cloves of garlic or a handful of chopped fresh herbs, to make a real change.

2 Drain the potatoes in a colander and return them to the pan. Add the butter, milk or cream and black pepper and use a potato masher to squash the spuds and flatten all the lumps. Add more milk if you like them really soft.

Cooking Rice

Measure rice in a jug, by volume rather than by weight, for best results.

Serves 2

INGREDIENTS
10 ml/2 tsp oil
150 ml/¼ pint/⅔ cup long grain
  white rice
300 ml/½ pint/1¼ cups boiling
  water or stock
salt

Cook's Tip
Some types of easy-cook rice may not take as long; check cooking times on the packet.

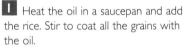

1 Heat the oil in a saucepan and add the rice. Stir to coat all the grains with the oil.

2 Pour on the boiling water or stock, add a little salt and stir once, before putting on the lid. Turn down the heat so the liquid is just simmering gently. Leave it alone for 15 minutes.

3 Lift the lid carefully (away from you) and check whether the rice is tender and that the liquid has almost gone. Fluff up the grains of rice with a fork and serve immediately.

Cooking Pasta

Pasta comes in loads of different shapes, sizes and colours. Green pasta has spinach in it, red pasta has tomato and brown pasta is made from wholemeal flour. Egg pasta has extra eggs in the dough. Allow about 115 g/4 oz dried pasta per person if it is the main ingredient, and a little less if it is to accompany a meal, although this may vary according to how hungry you are!

Serves 4

INGREDIENTS
350–450 g/12 oz–1 lb dried
  pasta
salt

COOK'S TIP
Fresh pasta is also available, but its cooking times are shorter – check pack instructions

2 Cook for 8–12 minutes, depending on what type of pasta you are using – spaghetti will not take as long as the thicker penne pasta. It should be al dente when cooked, which means it still has some firmness to it and isn't completely soft and soggy.

1 Bring a large saucepan of water to the boil. Add a little salt. Add the pasta to the pan, a little at a time, so that the water stays at a rolling boil.

3 Drain the pasta well in a colander and tip it back to the pan. Pour a sauce over or toss in a little melted butter.

Making Salad Dressing

Green or mixed salads add crunch and freshness to heavy, meaty meals like lasagne or barbecued ribs, but they are bland and boring without a dressing like this one.

Serves 4

INGREDIENTS
15 ml/1 tbsp white wine vinegar
10 ml/2 tsp coarse-grain
  mustard
salt
freshly ground black pepper
30 ml/2 tbsp oil

COOK'S TIP
Mix 30 ml/2 tbsp oil with 15 ml/ 1 tbsp lemon juice, for a tangier dressing. Add chopped fresh herbs for extra flavour.

1 Put the vinegar and mustard in a bowl or jug. Whisk well, then add a little salt and pepper.

2 Add the oil slowly, about 5 ml/1 tsp at a time, whisking constantly. Pour the dressing over the salad just before serving so that the lettuce stays crisp. Use two spoons to toss the salad and coat it with the dressing.

Skinny Dips

Jacket potatoes in disguise, with a delicious spicy dip.

Serves 4

INGREDIENTS
8 large potatoes, scrubbed
30–45 ml/2–3 tbsp oil
90 ml/6 tbsp mayonnaise
30 ml/2 tbsp natural yogurt
5 ml/1 tsp curry paste
30 ml/2 tbsp roughly chopped
  fresh coriander
salt

curry paste

potatoes

mayonnaise

fresh coriander

natural yogurt

1 Preheat the oven to 190°C/375°F/ Gas 5. Arrange the potatoes in a roasting tin, prick them all over with a fork and cook for 45 minutes, or until tender. Leave to cool slightly.

2 Carefully cut each potato into quarters lengthways, holding it with a clean tea towel if it's still a bit hot.

3 Scoop out some of the centre with a knife or spoon and put the skins back in the roasting tin. Save the cooked potato for making fish cakes.

4 Brush the skins with oil and sprinkle with salt before putting them back in the oven. Cook for 30–40 minutes more, until they are crisp and brown, brushing them occasionally with more oil.

5 Meanwhile, put the mayonnaise, yogurt, curry paste and 1 tbsp coriander in a small bowl and mix together well. Leave for 30–40 minutes for the flavour to develop.

6 Put the dip in a clean bowl and arrange the skins around the edge. Serve hot, sprinkled with the remaining coriander

COOK'S TIP
If there is just one of you, prick one large potato all over with a fork and microwave on HIGH for 6–8 minutes, until tender. Scoop out the centre, brush with oil and grill until browned.

Pile-it-High Mushrooms

Ideal for those vegetarians out there, this speedy snack is ideal on its own, or on toast or with crusty bread. If you're really starving, add a few prawn crackers.

Serves 4

INGREDIENTS

50 g/2 oz/¼ cup butter
2 garlic cloves, peeled and
  crushed
4 large flat mushrooms, peeled
  or wiped
2.5 cm/1 in piece fresh root
  ginger, grated
4 spring onions, cut in
  2.5 cm/1 in pieces
1 carrot, cut in matchsticks
6 baby sweetcorn, quartered
  lengthways
75 g/3 oz fine green beans,
  halved
30 ml/2 tbsp soy sauce
115 g/4 oz beansprouts, rinsed
  and drained

*fine
green beans*

*baby
sweetcorn*

*spring
onions*

*fresh
root ginger*

garlic

carrot

soy sauce

butter

flat mushrooms

beansprouts

1 Melt the butter in a large frying pan and fry the garlic until it has softened slightly. Put the mushrooms in the pan and fry gently for 8–10 minutes, turning once or twice, until tender. Lift out the mushrooms, place in a dish and cover to keep them hot.

2 Turn up the heat and add the ginger, spring onions, carrot, sweetcorn and beans to the pan and stir-fry for 2 minutes.

3 Add the soy sauce and beansprouts and cook for 1 minute more. Put each mushroom on a plate and top with the stir-fried vegetables. Serve immediately.

Nutty Chicken Kebabs

A tasty Thai starter that's quick to make and uses everyone's favourite spread in the dip.

Serves 4

INGREDIENTS
30 ml/2 tbsp oil
15 ml/1 tbsp lemon juice
450 g/1 lb boneless, skinless chicken breasts, cut in small cubes

FOR THE DIP
5 ml/1 tsp chilli powder
75 ml/5 tbsp water
15 ml/1 tbsp oil
1 small onion, grated
1 garlic clove, peeled and crushed
30 ml/2 tbsp lemon juice
60 ml/4 tbsp crunchy peanut butter
5 ml/1 tsp salt
5 ml/1 tsp ground coriander
sliced cucumber and lemon wedges, to serve

lemon juice

crunchy peanut butter

onion

oil

chilli powder

chicken

ground coriander

garlic

1 Soak 12 wooden skewers in water, to prevent them from burning during grilling. Mix the oil and lemon juice together in a bowl and stir in the cubed chicken. Cover and leave to marinate for at least 30 minutes.

2 Thread four or five cubes on each wooden skewer. Cook under a hot grill, turning often, until cooked and browned, about 10 minutes. Cut one piece open to check it is cooked right through: this is very important, especially for chicken.

3 Meanwhile, make the dip. Mix the chilli powder with 15 ml/1 tbsp of the water. Heat the oil in a small frying pan and fry the onion and garlic until tender.

4 Turn down the heat and add the chilli paste and the remaining ingredients and stir well. Stir in more water if the sauce is too thick and put it into a small bowl. Serve warm, with the chicken kebabs, cucumber slices and lemon wedges.

Super-duper Soup

Easy to make as there's no need to be too fussy – just chop up lots of your favourite vegetables and simmer them gently with tomatoes and stock. Serve with crusty bread.

Serves 4–6

INGREDIENTS
15 ml/1 tbsp oil
1 onion, sliced
2 carrots, sliced
675 g/1½ lb potatoes, cut in
   large chunks
1.2 litres/2 pints/5 cups
   vegetable stock
450 g/1 lb can chopped
   tomatoes
115 g/4 oz broccoli, cut in
   florets
1 courgette, sliced
115 g/4 oz mushrooms, sliced
7.5 ml/1½ tsp medium-hot
   curry powder (optional)
5 ml/1 tsp dried mixed herbs
salt and pepper

1 Heat the oil in a large saucepan and fry the onion and carrots gently, until they start to soften.

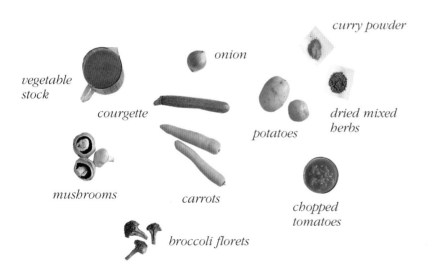

vegetable stock
courgette
mushrooms
carrots
onion
potatoes
curry powder
dried mixed herbs
chopped tomatoes
broccoli florets

2 Add the potatoes and fry gently for 2 minutes more; stir often or they might stick. Add the stock, tomatoes, broccoli, courgette and mushrooms.

3 Add the curry powder (if using), herbs and salt and pepper and bring to the boil. Put the lid on and simmer gently for 30–40 minutes, or until the vegetables are tender. Taste and add more salt and pepper if needed.

Cock-a-Noodle Soup

Take a tasty trip to the Far East, with this Chinese-style soup.

Serves 4–6

INGREDIENTS
15 ml/1 tbsp sesame oil
4 spring onions, roughly chopped
225 g/8 oz boneless, skinless chicken breasts, cut in small cubes
1.2 litres/2 pints/5 cups chicken stock
15 ml/1 tbsp soy sauce
115 g/4 oz/1 cup frozen sweetcorn niblets
115 g/4 oz medium thread egg-noodles
salt and pepper
1 carrot, thinly sliced lengthways, to garnish
prawn crackers, to serve (optional)

chicken stock

sweetcorn niblets

carrot

chicken

soy sauce

sesame oil

spring onions

thread egg-noodles

1 Heat the oil and fry the spring onions and chicken until the meat has browned all over.

2 Add the stock and the soy sauce and bring the soup to the boil.

3 Stir in the sweetcorn, then add the noodles, breaking them up roughly. Taste the soup and add salt and pepper if needed.

4 Use small cutters to stamp out shapes from the thin slices of carrot. Add them to the soup. Simmer for 5 minutes, before serving in bowls with prawn crackers, if you like.

See-in-the-Dark Soup

Stop stumbling around when the lights are off –
eat more carrots! Serve with crunchy toast.

Serves 4

INGREDIENTS
15 ml/1 tbsp oil
1 onion, sliced
450 g/1 lb carrots, sliced
75 g/3 oz/½ cup split red lentils
1.2 litres/2 pints/5 cups
  vegetable stock
5 ml/1 tsp ground coriander
75 ml/3 tbsp chopped fresh
  parsley
salt and pepper

vegetable stock

onion

parsley

red lentils

carrots

ground coriander

1 Heat the oil and fry the onion until it is starting to brown. Add the sliced carrots and fry gently for 4–5 minutes, stirring them often, until they soften.

3 Add the lentils, stock and coriander to the saucepan with a little salt and pepper. Bring the soup to the boil.

2 Meanwhile, put the lentils in a small bowl and cover with cold water. Pour off any bits that float. Tip the lentils into a sieve and rinse under the cold tap.

4 Turn down the heat, put the lid on and leave to simmer gently for 30 minutes, or until the lentils are cooked.

5 Add the chopped parsley and cook for 5 minutes more. Remove from the heat and allow to cool slightly.

6 Carefully put the soup into a food processor or blender and whizz until it is smooth. (You may have to do this a half at a time.) Rinse the saucepan before pouring the soup back in and add a little water if it looks too thick. Heat up again before serving.

COOK'S TIP
Push the soup through a sieve with a wooden spoon or leave it chunky, if you don't have a food processor or blender.

Tasty Toasts

Next time friends come over to watch a video, surprise them with these delicious treats.

Serves 4

INGREDIENTS
2 red peppers, halved length-ways and seeded
30 ml/2 tbsp oil
1 garlic clove, peeled and crushed
1 French baton (short French stick)
45 ml/3 tbsp pesto
50 g/2 oz/⅓ cup French soft goat's cheese

garlic

French baton   *soft goat's cheese*

red peppers

pesto

oil

I Put the pepper halves, cut-side down, under a hot grill and let the skins blacken. Carefully put the halves in a plastic bag, tie the top and leave them until they are cool enough to handle. Peel off the skins and cut the peppers into strips.

2 Put the oil in a small bowl and stir in the garlic. Cut the bread into slanting slices and brush one side with the garlic-flavoured oil. Arrange the slices on a grill pan and brown under a hot grill.

3 Turn the slices over and brush the untoasted sides with the garlic-flavoured oil and then with the pesto.

4 Arrange pepper strips over each slice and put small wedges of goat's cheese on top. Put back under the grill and toast until the cheese has browned and melted slightly. Serve hot or cold.

Chilli Cheese Nachos

Viva Mexico! Silence that hungry tummy with a truly spicy snack. Make it as cool or as hot as you like, by adjusting the amount of sliced jalapeno peppers. Ole!

Serves 4

INGREDIENTS
115 g/4 oz bag chilli tortilla
    chips
50 g/2 oz Cheddar cheese,
    grated
50 g/2 oz Red Leicester cheese,
    grated
50 g/2 oz pickled green
    jalapeno chillies, sliced

FOR THE DIP
30 ml/2 tbsp lemon juice
1 avocado, roughly chopped
1 beefsteak tomato, roughly
    chopped
salt and pepper

1 Arrange the tortilla chips in an even layer on a flameproof plate which can be used under the grill. Sprinkle all the grated cheese over and then scatter as many jalapeno chillies as you like over the top.

beefsteak tomato

pickled green
jalapeno
chillies

grated Cheddar
cheese

avocado

lemon juice

chilli tortilla
chips

grated Red
Leicester cheese

2 Put the plate under a hot grill and toast until the cheese has melted and browned – keep an eye on the chips to make sure they don't burn.

3 Mix the lemon juice, avocado and tomato together in a bowl. Add salt and pepper to taste and serve with the chips.

Wicked Tortilla Wedges

A tortilla is a thick omelette with lots of cooked potatoes in it. It is very popular in Spain, where it is cut in thick slices like a cake and served with bread. Try it with sliced tomato salad.

Serves 4

INGREDIENTS

30 ml/2 tbsp oil
675 g/1½ lb potatoes, cut in small chunks
1 onion, sliced
115 g/4 oz mushrooms, sliced
115 g/4 oz/1 cup frozen peas, thawed
50 g/2 oz/⅓ cup frozen sweetcorn niblets, thawed
4 eggs
150 ml/¼ pint/⅔ cup milk
10 ml/2 tsp Cajun seasoning
30 ml/2 tbsp chopped fresh parsley
salt and pepper

milk *sweetcorn*

mushrooms *parsley*

eggs *potatoes*

Cajun seasoning *peas*

onion

1 Heat the oil in a large frying pan and fry the potatoes and onion for 3–4 minutes, stirring often. Turn down the heat, cover the pan and fry gently for another 8–10 minutes, until the potatoes are almost tender.

2 Add the mushrooms to the pan and cook for 2–3 minutes more, stirring often, until they have softened.

3 Add the peas and sweetcorn and stir them into the potato mixture.

4 Put the eggs, milk and Cajun seasoning in a bowl. Add salt and pepper to taste and beat well.

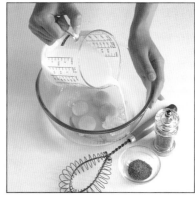

5 Level the top of the vegetables and scatter the parsley on top. Pour the egg mixture over and cook over a low heat for 10–15 minutes.

6 Put the pan under a hot grill to set the top of the tortilla. Serve hot or cold, cut into wedges.

COOK'S TIP
Use less Cajun seasoning if you don't like spicy food. Make sure the frying pan can be used under the grill.

Give 'em a Roasting

Don't stick to roast spuds! A good roasting brings out the colours and flavours of other vegetables too.

Serves 4

INGREDIENTS
1 aubergine, cut in large chunks
15 ml/1 tbsp salt
1 red pepper, seeded and cut in thick strips
1 green pepper, seeded and cut in thick strips
1 yellow pepper, seeded and cut in thick strips
1 courgette, cut in large chunks
1 onion, cut in thick slices
115 g/4 oz small mushrooms
225 g/8 oz plum tomatoes, quartered
75 ml/5 tbsp olive oil
4–5 thyme sprigs
2 oregano sprigs
3–4 rosemary sprigs
sea salt and freshly ground black pepper

peppers *thyme* *aubergine*

onion *oil* *rosemary*

courgette *plum tomatoes*

mushrooms *oregano*

1 Arrange the aubergine chunks on a plate and sprinkle them with the salt. Leave for 30 minutes.

2 Squeeze the aubergine to remove as much liquid as possible. Rinse off the salt. This process stops the aubergine tasting so bitter.

3 Preheat the oven to 200°C/400°F/ Gas 6. Arrange all the vegetables, including the aubergine, in a roasting tin and drizzle the oil over.

4 Scatter most of the herb sprigs in amongst the vegetables and season well. Put the tin into the hot oven and cook for 20–25 minutes.

5 Turn the vegetables over and cook them for 15 minutes more, or until they are tender and browned.

6 Scatter the remaining fresh herb sprigs over the cooked vegetables just before serving.

Chunky Cheesy Salad

Something to really sink your teeth into – this salad is choc-a-bloc with vitamins and energy. Serve on large slices of crusty bread.

Serves 4

INGREDIENTS
¼ small white cabbage, finely chopped
¼ small red cabbage, finely chopped
8 baby carrots, thinly sliced
50 g/2 oz small mushrooms, quartered
115 g/4 oz cauliflower, cut in small florets
1 small courgette, grated
10 cm/4 in piece cucumber, cubed
2 tomatoes, roughly chopped
50 g/2 oz sprouted seeds
50 g/2 oz/½ cup salted peanuts
30 ml/2 tbsp sunflower oil
15 ml/1 tbsp lemon juice
salt and pepper
50 g/2 oz cheese, grated

1 Put all the prepared vegetables and the sprouted seeds in a bowl and mix together well.

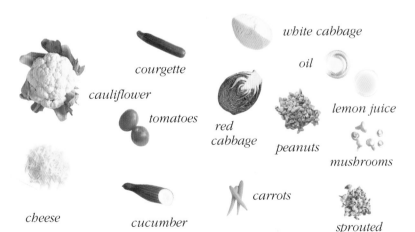

white cabbage
courgette
oil
cauliflower
lemon juice
tomatoes
red cabbage
peanuts
mushrooms
cheese
cucumber
carrots
sprouted seeds

2 Stir in the peanuts. Drizzle the oil and lemon juice over. Season well and leave to stand for 30 minutes to allow the flavour to develop.

3 Sprinkle grated cheese over just before serving on large slices of crusty bread. Have extra dressing ready, in case anybody wants more.

Yellow Chicken

An all-time Chinese favourite that you can stir-fry in a few minutes. Serve with boiled rice.

Serves 4

INGREDIENTS
30 ml/2 tbsp oil
75 g/3 oz/¾ cup salted cashew
  nuts
4 spring onions, roughly
  chopped
450 g/1 lb boneless, skinless
  chicken breasts, cut in strips
165 g/5½ oz jar yellow bean
  sauce

yellow bean sauce

spring onions

chicken

cashew nuts

oil

1 Heat 15 ml/1 tbsp of the oil in a frying pan and fry the cashew nuts until browned. This does not take long, so keep an eye on them. Lift them out with a slotted spoon and put them to one side.

2 Heat the remaining oil and fry the spring onions and chicken for 5–8 minutes, until the meat is browned all over and cooked.

3 Return the nuts to the pan and pour the jar of sauce over. Stir well and cook gently until hot. Serve at once.

COOK'S TIP

Cashew nuts are quite expensive, but you can buy broken cashews, which are cheaper and perfectly good for this dish. You could also use almonds, if you prefer.

Pepperoni Pasta

Add extra zip to bland and boring pasta dishes with spicy pepperoni sausage.

Serves 4

INGREDIENTS
275 g/10 oz/2½ cups dried pasta
175 g/6 oz pepperoni sausage, sliced
1 small or ½ large red onion, sliced
45 ml/3 tbsp green pesto
150 ml/¼ pint/⅔ cup double cream
225 g/8 oz cherry tomatoes, halved
15 g/½ oz fresh chives
salt

cherry tomatoes

green pesto

pasta

double cream

fresh chives

red onion

pepperoni sausage

1 Cook the pasta in a large pan of lightly salted, boiling water, following the instructions on the packet.

2 Meanwhile, gently fry the pepperoni sausage slices and the onion together in a frying pan until the onion is soft. The oil from the sausage will mean you won't need extra oil.

3 Mix the pesto sauce and cream together in a small bowl.

4 Add this mixture to the frying pan and stir until the sauce is smooth.

5 Add the cherry tomatoes and snip the chives over the top with scissors. Stir again.

6 Drain the pasta and tip it back into the pan. Pour the sauce over and mix well, making sure all the pasta is coated. Serve immediately.

COOK'S TIP
Use a mixture of red and yellow cherry tomatoes for a really colourful meal. Serve with sesame bread sticks.

Pancake Parcels

Be adventurous with your pancakes! Don't just stick to lemon and sugar: try this savoury version for a real change.

Serves 4

INGREDIENTS
FOR THE PANCAKES
115 g/4 oz/1 cup plain flour
1 egg
300 ml/½ pint/1¼ cups milk
2.5 ml/½ tsp salt
25 g/1 oz/2 tbsp butter,
  for frying

FOR THE FILLING
200 g/7 oz/scant 1 cup cream
  cheese with chives
90 ml/6 tbsp double cream
115 g/4 oz ham, cut in strips
115 g/4 oz cheese, grated
15 g/½ oz/¼ cup fresh
  breadcrumbs
salt and pepper

breadcrumbs

butter

cream

flour

cheese

milk

ham

cream cheese with chives

egg

1 To make the pancakes, put the flour, egg, a little milk and the salt in a bowl and beat together with a wooden spoon. Gradually beat in the rest of the milk until the batter looks like double cream. (The milk must be added slowly or the batter will be lumpy.)

2 Melt a little butter in a medium-size frying pan and pour in just enough batter to cover the base in a thin layer. Tilt and turn the pan to spread the batter out. Cook gently until set, then turn over with a palette knife and cook the second side. If you feel brave enough try tossing the pancakes!

3 Slide the pancake out of the pan. Stack them in a pile, with a piece of greaseproof paper between each one to stop them sticking to each other. There should be enough batter to make four large pancakes. Preheat the oven to 190°C/375°F/Gas 5.

4 Make the filling. Beat the cream cheese and cream in a bowl. Add the ham and half the cheese; season well. Put a spoonful of the mixture in the centre of a pancake.

5 Fold one side over the mixture and then the other. Fold both ends up as well to make a small parcel. Arrange the parcels on a baking sheet, with the joins underneath. Make three more parcels in the same way.

6 Sprinkle the remaining cheese and the breadcrumbs over the parcels and cover with foil. Cook for 20 minutes. Remove the foil. Cook for 10 minutes more, until browned. Tie green spring onion around the parcels, if you like.

Eggs in a Blanket

A hearty brunch or lunch to tuck into on a chilly day, with chunks of wholemeal bread.

Serves 4

INGREDIENTS
1 aubergine, sliced
5 ml/1 tsp salt
15 ml/1 tbsp oil
1 onion, sliced
1 garlic clove, crushed
1 yellow pepper, seeded and
   sliced
1 courgette, sliced
400 g/14 oz can chopped
   tomatoes
120 ml/4 fl oz/½ cup water
10 ml/2 tsp dried mixed herbs
4 eggs
salt and pepper

aubergine

pepper   *salt*
      courgette

chopped
tomatoes

                 eggs
      garlic
onion

mixed
herbs

1 Arrange the aubergine slices on a plate, sprinkle with salt and leave for 30 minutes. Rinse and squeeze out as much juice as you can.

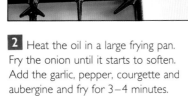

2 Heat the oil in a large frying pan. Fry the onion until it starts to soften. Add the garlic, pepper, courgette and aubergine and fry for 3–4 minutes.

3 Add the chopped tomatoes, water and herbs. Stir in salt and pepper to taste. Simmer gently for 5 minutes.

4 Make four shallow dips in the mixture and break an egg into each one. Cover the pan with a lid or foil and simmer for 8–12 minutes, until the eggs are set and the vegetables are tender.

Chicken Crisp

Forget all that spud-bashing – top your pie with a packet of crisps instead.

Serves 4

INGREDIENTS
115 g/4 oz/1 cup dried pasta
　shapes
175 g/6 oz broccoli, cut in
　florets
50 g/2 oz/¼ cup butter
1 red onion, thinly sliced
4 streaky bacon rashers,
　chopped
225 g/8 oz boneless, skinless
　chicken breasts, cut in chunks
60 ml/4 tbsp plain flour
450 ml/¾ pint/scant 2 cups milk
salt and pepper

FOR THE TOPPING
3 small packets of crisps
75 g/3 oz cheese, grated

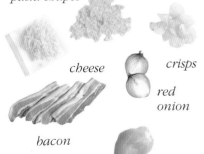

butter

flour

milk

broccoli

pasta shapes

cheese

crisps

red onion

bacon

chicken

1 Cook the pasta in lightly salted, boiling water for 5 minutes. Add the broccoli and cook for 5 minutes more, until the pasta and broccoli are tender. Drain well.

2 Meanwhile, melt the butter in a saucepan and fry the onion until it starts to soften. Add the bacon and chicken and fry gently until browned all over. Add the flour and mix well.

3 Lift the pan off the heat and very gradually mix in the milk. Season, return to the heat and bring to the boil, stirring all the time. Stir in the drained pasta and broccoli. Tip the mixture into a dish that can go under a grill.

4 Preheat the grill. Cover the top of the mixture with the crisps and sprinkle with the cheese. Put under the hot grill for a few minutes, until the cheese has melted and browned.

Something Very Fishy

If you like getting your hands messy, this is the recipe for you! Serve with green vegetables and new potatoes.

Serves 4

INGREDIENTS
450 g/1 lb old potatoes, cut in small chunks
25 g/1 oz/2 tbsp butter
15 ml/1 tbsp milk
412 g/14½ oz can pink salmon, drained, skinned and boned
1 egg, beaten
60 ml/4 tbsp plain flour
2 spring onions, finely chopped
4 sun-dried tomatoes in oil, chopped
grated rind of 1 lemon
oil, for frying
25 g/1 oz sesame seeds
salt and pepper

salmon

butter

potatoes

milk

egg

flour

spring onions

lemon

sesame seeds

sun-dried tomatoes

1 Cook the potatoes in boiling, lightly salted water until tender. Drain and return to the saucepan. Add the butter and milk and mash until smooth. Season well.

2 Put the mashed potato in a bowl and beat in the salmon. Add the egg, flour, spring onions, tomatoes and lemon rind. Mix well.

3 Divide the mixture into eight equal pieces and pat them into fish cake shapes, using floured hands.

4 Put the sesame seeds on a large plate and very gently press both sides of the fish cakes into them, until the cakes are lightly coated.

5 Pour oil into a frying pan to a depth of about 1 cm/½ in. Heat it gently. Put a small cube of bread in the pan and, if it sizzles, the oil is ready to cook the fish cakes. You will need to cook the fish cakes in several batches.

6 When one side is crisp and brown turn the cakes over carefully with a spatula and a fork, to cook the second side. The fish cakes are quite soft and need gentle treatment or they will break up. Lift them out and put them aside to drain on kitchen paper. Keep hot until they are all cooked.

COOK'S TIP
Use canned tuna instead of the salmon, if you prefer.

Sticky Fingers

You have to like messy food to eat this popular dish, so plenty of napkins please! Juicy tomatoes make a refreshing accompaniment.

Serves 4

INGREDIENTS
30 ml/2 tbsp oil
1 onion, chopped
1 garlic clove, crushed
30 ml/2 tbsp tomato purée
15 ml/1 tbsp white wine vinegar
45 ml/3 tbsp clear honey
5 ml/1 tsp dried mixed herbs
2.5 ml/½ tsp chilli powder
150 ml/¼ pint/⅔ cup chicken
   stock
8 chicken thighs
350 g/12 oz spare ribs

FOR THE POTATOES
675 g/1½ lb potatoes, cubed
30 ml/2 tbsp oil
1 large onion, sliced
1 garlic clove, crushed
salt and pepper

chicken
stock

onion

tomato
purée

spare ribs

chilli
powder

potatoes

vinegar

honey

garlic

chicken
thighs

mixed herbs

1 Heat the oil in a saucepan and fry the onion and garlic until the onion starts to soften.

2 Add the tomato purée, vinegar, honey, herbs, chilli powder and stock and bring to the boil. Lower the heat and simmer for 15–20 minutes, when the sauce should have thickened.

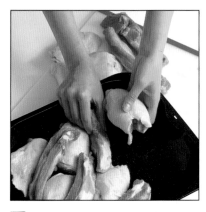

3 Preheat the oven to 190°C/375°F/Gas 5. Arrange the chicken and ribs in a roasting tin.

4 Spoon the sauce evenly over the meat and cook for 30 minutes. Turn the meat over to ensure that it is coated evenly in the sauce.

5 Cook for 45 minutes more, turning the meat several times and spooning the sauce over. The meat should be really browned and sticky.

6 Meanwhile, put the potatoes in lightly salted water, bring to the boil, then drain well. Heat the oil in a large frying pan. Fry the onion until it starts to turn brown. Add the potatoes and garlic and fry for 25–30 minutes, until everything is cooked through, browned and crisp.

Tiny Toads

Serve these pint-sized portions of toad-in-the-hole with peas.

Serves 4

INGREDIENTS
115 g/4 oz/1 cup plain flour
1 egg
300 ml/½ pint/1¼ cups milk
45 ml/3 tbsp fresh mixed herbs,
  e.g. parsley, thyme and chives,
  roughly chopped
24 cocktail sausages
salt and pepper

FOR THE ONION GRAVY
15 ml/1 tbsp oil
2 onions, sliced
600 ml/1 pint/2½ cups stock
15 ml/1 tbsp soy sauce
15 ml/1 tbsp whole-grain
  mustard
30 ml/2 tbsp cornflour
30 ml/2 tbsp water

stock

milk

onions

mustard

sausages

soy sauce

flour　*cornflour*　*chives*

thyme

egg　*parsley*

1 Preheat the oven to 200°C/400°F/Gas 6. Put the flour, egg and a little milk in a bowl and mix well with a wooden spoon. Gradually mix in the rest of the milk to make a batter. Season well with salt and pepper and stir in the herbs.

2 Lightly oil eight 10 cm/4 in non-stick Yorkshire pudding tins and arrange three sausages in each. Cook in the hot oven for 10 minutes.

COOK'S TIP

Use vegetarian sausages for friends who don't eat meat.

3 Carefully take the tins out of the oven and use a ladle to pour batter into each tin. Put them back in the oven and cook for 30–40 minutes more, until the batter is risen and browned.

4 Meanwhile, heat the oil in a pan. Fry the onions for 15 minutes until really browned. Add the stock, soy and mustard and bring to the boil. Mix the cornflour and water together in a cup and pour into the gravy. Bring to the boil, stirring. Serve with the "toads".

Cherry Tomato Coca

This looks rather like a pizza but tastes very different.

Serves 4

INGREDIENTS

225 g/8 oz/2 cups strong white
  flour
5 ml/1 tsp salt
6 g/¼ oz sachet easy-blend yeast
200 ml/7 fl oz/scant 1 cup
  hand-hot water
1 egg, beaten
45 ml/3 tbsp poppy seeds
2 red peppers, seeded and cut
  in strips
1 red onion, cut in strips
225 g/8 oz cherry tomatoes,
  halved
45 ml/3 tbsp olive oil
salt and pepper
fresh basil leaves, to garnish

flour

water

peppers

basil

egg

tomatoes

poppy seeds

red onion

yeast

olive oil

1 Put the flour, salt and yeast in a bowl and mix well. Add half the water and mix with a knife. Add the rest of the water and use your hands to pull the mixture together to make a dough.

2 Put the dough on a lightly floured surface and knead for 5 minutes, until it is no longer sticky but smooth and stretchy. Put in a bowl, cover with clear film and leave for 30–45 minutes in a warm place, such as an airing cupboard, until doubled in size.

3 Meanwhile, preheat the oven to 200°C/400°F/Gas 6. Knead the dough again and roll or press it out into a rectangular shape about 5 mm/¼ in thick. Put it on a baking sheet and brush the edges with the beaten egg. Sprinkle the edges with poppy seeds. Scatter the prepared vegetables on the unseeded central area and drizzle the oil over the top. Sprinkle with salt and pepper and cook for 30–40 minutes, until the dough has risen and browned and the vegetables have cooked. Garnish with basil and serve hot or cold.

Raving Ravioli

Have a raving good time making your own
pasta – get your friends to help.

Serves 4

INGREDIENTS
75 g/3 oz fresh spinach, torn
  up, with tough stalks removed
275 g/10 oz/2½ cups strong
  white flour
3 eggs, beaten
15 ml/1 tbsp oil
salt and pepper
300 ml/½ pint/1¼ cups
  double cream
15ml/1 tbsp chopped fresh
  coriander
30 ml/2 tbsp grated Parmesan
  cheese, plus extra to serve

FOR THE FILLING
115 g/4 oz trout fillet, poached
  and drained, skin and bones
  removed
50 g/2 oz/⅓ cup ricotta cheese
grated rind of 1 lemon
30 ml/1 tbsp chopped fresh
  coriander
salt and pepper

eggs

cream   *spinach*

oil

trout fillet

flour   *lemon*

Parmesan cheese   *ricotta cheese*

fresh coriander

1 Steam the spinach over a pan of boiling water until it wilts. Allow to cool, and squeeze out as much water as you can. Put it into a food processor, with the flour, eggs, oil and salt and pepper and whizz until the mixture forms a dough.

2 Place the dough on a lightly floured surface and knead it for 5 minutes, until smooth. Wrap it in clear film and chill in the fridge for 30 minutes.

3 Sprinkle the work surface with flour. Roll out the dough to make a 50 x 46 cm/20 x 18 in shape, so the dough is the thickness of card. Leave to dry for 15 minutes. Use a sharp knife or pastry wheel to trim the edges and cut the dough in half.

4 Put the trout in a small bowl. Add the ricotta cheese, lemon rind, the coriander and salt and pepper and beat together. Put four spoonfuls of the filling across the top of the dough, leaving a small border round the edge. Carry on putting the filling mixture in lines, to make eight rows. Lift up the second sheet of pasta on a rolling pin and lay it gently over the first sheet.

5 Run your finger between the bumps to remove any air and to press the dough together. Using a knife or pastry wheel, cut the ravioli into small parcels and trim round the edge as well, to seal each one. Cook in lightly salted boiling water for 8–10 minutes. Drain and return to the pan.

6 Put the cream, remaining coriander and the Parmesan in a small saucepan and heat gently, without boiling. Pour over the ravioli and stir until evenly coated. Serve immediately, garnished with a sprig of coriander and Parmesan. Hand extra Parmesan round, if you like.

Homeburgers

These look the same as ordinary burgers, but watch out for the soft, cheesy centre. Serve with chips and sliced tomatoes.

Serves 4

INGREDIENTS

450 g/1 lb lean minced beef
2 slices of bread, crusts removed
1 egg
4 spring onions, roughly chopped
1 garlic clove, peeled and chopped
15 ml/1 tbsp mango chutney
10 ml/2 tsp dried mixed herbs
50 g/2 oz/⅓ cup mozzarella cheese
salt and pepper
4 burger buns, to serve

minced beef

bread

spring onions

mozzarella cheese

egg

garlic

mango chutney

mixed herbs

1 Put the mince, bread, egg, spring onions and garlic in a food processor. Add a little salt and pepper and whizz until evenly blended. Add the chutney and herbs and whizz again.

2 Divide the mixture into four equal portions and pat flat, with damp hands, to stop the meat from sticking.

3 Cut the cheese into four equal pieces and put one in the centre of each piece of beef. Wrap the meat round the cheese to make a fat burger. Chill for 30 minutes. Preheat the grill.

4 Put the burgers on a rack under the hot grill, but not too close or they will burn on the outside before the middle has cooked properly. Cook them for 5–8 minutes on each side then put each burger in a roll, with your favourite trimmings.

Popeye's Pie

Tuck into this layered pie and you, too, can have bulging muscles!

Serves 4

INGREDIENTS
75 g/3 oz/⅓ cup butter
5 ml/1 tsp grated nutmeg
900 g/2 lb fresh spinach, washed and large stalks removed
115 g/4 oz/⅔ cup feta cheese, crumbled
50 g/2 oz Cheddar cheese, grated
275 g/10 oz filo pastry sheets
10 ml/2 tsp mixed ground cinnamon, nutmeg and black pepper

spinach

filo pastry

feta cheese

black pepper

cinnamon

nutmeg

butter

Cheddar cheese

1 Melt 25 g/1 oz/2 tbsp of the butter in a large frying pan, add the nutmeg and the spinach and season well. Cover and cook for 5 minutes, or until the spinach is tender. Drain well, pressing out as much liquid as possible.

2 Preheat the oven to 160°C/325°F/ Gas 3. Melt the remaining butter in a small saucepan. Mix the cheeses together in a bowl and season them with salt and pepper. Unfold the pastry so the sheets are flat. Use one to line part of the base of a small, deep-sided, greased roasting tin. Brush with melted butter. Keep the remaining filo sheets covered with a damp tea towel: they dry out very quickly.

3 Continue to lay pastry sheets across the base and up the sides of the tin, brushing each time with butter, until two-thirds of the pastry has been used. Don't worry if they flop over the top edges – they will be tidied up later.

4 Mix together the grated cheeses and spinach and spread them into the tin. Fold the pastry edges over. Crumple up the remaining sheets of pastry and arrange them over the top of the filling. Brush with melted butter and sprinkle the mixed spices over the top. Cook the pie for 45 minutes. Raise the oven temperature to 200°C/400°F/Gas 6, for 10–15 minutes more, to brown the top.

Turkey Surprise Packages

This looks just like a paper parcel but there's a special treat inside. Put a parcel on each plate, with new potatoes and green vegetables, and let everyone open their own surprise.

Serves 4

INGREDIENTS
30 ml/2 tbsp chopped parsley
4 turkey breast steaks, weighing
   150–175 g/5–6 oz each
8 streaky bacon rashers
2 spring onions, cut in thin
   strips
50 g/2 oz fennel, cut in thin
   strips
1 carrot, cut in thin strips
1 small celery stick, cut in thin
   strips
grated rind and juice of 1 lemon
salt and pepper
lemon wedges, to serve

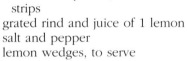

celery
lemon
spring onions
fennel
carrot
turkey
bacon
parsley

1 Pat parsley over each turkey breast steak, then wrap two rashers of bacon round each one.

2 Preheat the oven to 190°C/375°F/Gas 5. Cut four 30 cm/12 in circles out of baking parchment or greaseproof paper and put a turkey breast just off centre on each one.

3 Arrange the vegetable strips on top of the steaks, sprinkle the lemon rind and juice over and season well with salt and pepper.

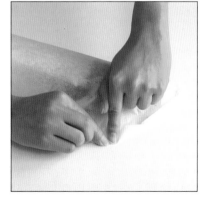

4 Fold the paper over the meat and vegetables and, starting at one side, twist and fold the paper edges together.

5 Work your way round the semi-circle, to seal the edges of the parcel together neatly.

6 Put all four parcels in a roasting tin and cook for 35–45 minutes, or until the meat is cooked and tender. Check that the steaks are cooked right through. Serve the packages with the lemon wedges to squeeze over them.

Fish 'n' Rice

This tasty paella-type meal uses a frozen fish mixture that saves lots of preparation time.

Serves 4

INGREDIENTS
30 ml/2 tbsp oil
1 onion, sliced
1 red pepper, seeded and
  chopped
115 g/4 oz mushrooms,
  chopped
10 ml/2 tsp ground turmeric
225 g/8 oz/scant 1½ cups rice
  and grain mix (or rice)
750 ml/1¼ pints/3 cups stock,
  made with a pilau-rice stock
  cube
400 g/14 oz bag frozen
  premium seafood selection,
  thawed
115 g/4 oz frozen large tiger
  prawns, thawed
salt and pepper

pepper *onion* *mixed grains*

stock *seafood selection* *oil*

turmeric

tiger prawns *mushrooms*

1 Heat the oil in a deep frying pan and fry the onion until it is starting to soften. Add the chopped pepper and mushrooms and fry for 1 minute.

2 Stir in the turmeric and then the grains. Stir until well mixed, then carefully pour on the stock. Season with salt and pepper, cover with a lid or foil and leave to simmer gently for 15 minutes.

3 Add the seafood selection and the prawns, stir well and turn up the heat slightly to bring the liquid back to the boil. Cover again and simmer for 15–20 minutes more, until the grains are cooked and the fish is hot. Serve the fish immediately.

COOK'S TIP

If you don't like this fish mixture, choose your own – use more prawns and crab sticks if you prefer, but cut down on the fish cooking time.

Honey Chops

These tasty sticky chops are very quick and easy to prepare and grill, but they would be just as good barbecued. Serve with herby mashed potatoes or chips.

Serves 4

INGREDIENTS
450 g/1 lb carrots
15 ml/1 tbsp butter
15 ml/1 tbsp soft brown sugar
15 ml/1 tbsp sesame seeds

FOR THE CHOPS
4 pork loin chops
50 g/2 oz/¼ cup butter
30 ml/2 tbsp clear honey
15 ml/1 tbsp tomato purée

carrots   honey

butter

tomato purée

pork loin chops

sesame seeds

soft brown sugar

COOK'S TIP

If the chops are very thick, put under a medium-hot grill for longer to make sure the chops are cooked in the middle.

1 Cut the carrots into matchstick shapes, put them in a saucepan and just cover them with cold water. Add the butter and brown sugar and bring to the boil. Turn down the heat and leave to simmer for 15–20 minutes, until most of the liquid has boiled away.

2 Line the grill pan with foil and arrange the pork chops on the grill rack. Beat the butter and honey together and gradually beat in the tomato purée, to make a smooth paste. Preheat the grill to high.

3 Spread half the honey paste over the chops and grill them for 5 minutes, until browned.

4 Carefully turn the chops over, spread them with the remaining honey paste and return to the grill. Grill the second side for a further 5 minutes, or until the meat is cooked through. Sprinkle the sesame seeds over the carrots and serve with the chops.

Bo Peep's Favourite

Racks of lamb are actually lamb chops, called "best end", that are still joined together.

Serves 4

INGREDIENTS
2 racks of lamb, with at least
  four chops in each piece
25 g/1 oz/2 tbsp butter
4 spring onions, roughly
  chopped
115 g/4 oz/⅔ cup basmati rice
300 ml/½ pint/1¼ cups stock
1 large ripe mango, peeled and
  roughly chopped
salt and pepper

FOR THE ROAST POTATOES
900 g/2 lb potatoes, peeled and
  cut in large, even pieces
30 ml/2 tbsp oil
15 ml/1 tbsp coarse sea salt

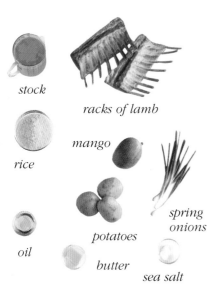

stock

racks of lamb

mango

rice

potatoes

spring
onions

oil

butter

sea salt

COOK'S TIP
Tell your butcher that you are cooking a "Guard of Honour" and he will prepare the meat for you. Serve with minty peas.

1 Use a sharp knife to cut the meat off the ends of the bones. Discard the thick, fatty skin and scrape the bones as clean as possible. Chop the trimmings into small pieces and save them for the stuffing. (The butcher can do all this, if you prefer.)

4 Remove from the heat, stir in the mango and taste the stuffing. Add salt and pepper. Preheat the oven to 190°C/375°F/Gas 5.

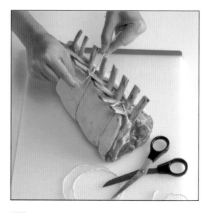

2 Interlock the bones like fingers and tie the two sides together with a piece of string between each two chops. Stand them in a roasting tin.

5 Put the stuffing in the middle of the chops. Wrap the ends of the bones in a thin strip of foil and put the tin in the oven. Cook for 30 minutes.

3 Melt the butter in a saucepan, add the spring onions and lamb trimmings and fry until the meat has browned. Add the rice, stir well and pour in the stock. Bring to the boil, lower the heat, put a lid on the pan and leave to simmer for 8–10 minutes, until the rice is tender.

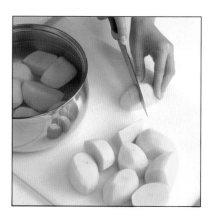

6 While the meat is cooking, make deep cuts in the rounded side of each potato and put them in a saucepan with cold, salted water. Bring to the boil. Drain and arrange round the outside of the meat. Drizzle the oil over, sprinkle with sea salt and return to oven for 1–1½ hours, until the potatoes are crisp and the meat is cooked.

Chocolate Puffs

These are always a firm favourite and so easy and cheap to make.

Serves 4–6

INGREDIENTS
150 ml/¼ pint/⅔ cup water
50 g/2 oz/¼ cup butter
65 g/2½ oz/generous ½ cup
   plain flour, sifted
2 eggs, beaten

FOR THE FILLING AND ICING
150 ml/¼ pint/⅔ cup double
   cream
225 g/8 oz/1½ cups icing sugar
15 ml/1 tbsp cocoa powder
30–60 ml/2–4 tbsp water

flour

water

cream

*icing
sugar*

*cocoa
powder*

butter

eggs

1 Put the water in a saucepan, add the butter and heat gently until it melts. Bring to the boil and remove from the heat. Tip in all the flour at once and beat quickly until the mixture sticks together, leaving the side of the pan clean. Leave to cool slightly.

2 Add the eggs, a little at a time, to the mixture and beat well each time, by hand with a wooden spoon or with an electric whisk, until the mixture is thick and glossy and drops reluctantly from a spoon (you may not need to use all of the egg). Preheat the oven to 220°C/425°F/Gas 7.

3 Dampen two baking sheets with cold water and put walnut-sized spoonfuls of the mixture on them. Leave some space for them to rise. Cook for 25–30 minutes, until they are golden brown and well risen. Use a palette knife to lift them on to a wire rack and make a small hole in each one with the handle of a wooden spoon to allow the steam to escape. Leave to cool.

4 Make the filling and icing. Whip the cream until thick. Put it into a piping bag fitted with a plain or star nozzle. Push the nozzle into the hole in each puff and squirt a little cream inside. Put the icing sugar and cocoa in a small bowl and stir together. Add enough water to make a thick glossy icing. Spread a spoonful of icing on each puff and serve.

COOK'S TIP

If the unfilled profiteroles go soggy, put them back into a hot oven for a few minutes and they will crisp up again.

Let's Get Tropical

Supermarkets are full of weird and wonderful fruits that make a really tangy salad when mixed together. Serve with cream or yogurt.

Serves 4

INGREDIENTS
1 small pineapple
2 kiwi fruit
1 ripe mango
1 watermelon slice
2 peaches
2 bananas
60 ml/4 tbsp tropical fruit juice

tropical fruit juice

watermelon

mango

pineapple

peaches   *kiwi fruit*   *bananas*

1 Cut the pineapple into 1 cm/½ in slices. Work round the edge of each slice, cutting off the skin and any spiky bits. Cut each slice into wedges and put them in a bowl.

2 Use a potato peeler to remove the skin from the kiwi fruit. Cut them in half lengthways and then into wedges. Add to the fruit bowl.

3 Cut the mango lengthways into quarters and cut round the large flat stone. Peel the flesh and cut it into chunks or slices.

4 Cut the watermelon into slices, cut off the skin and cut the flesh into chunks. Remove the seeds. Cut the peaches in half, remove the stones and cut the flesh into wedges. Slice the bananas. Add all the fruit to the bowl and gently stir in the fruit juice.

Monster Meringues

A mouth-watering dessert made from meringue,
whipped cream and tangy summer fruits.

Serves 4

Ingredients

3 egg whites
175 g/6 oz/¾ cup caster sugar
15 ml/1 tbsp cornflour
5 ml/1 tsp white wine vinegar
few drops vanilla essence
225 g/8 oz assorted red summer
    fruits
300 ml/½ pint/1¼ cups
    double cream
1 passion fruit

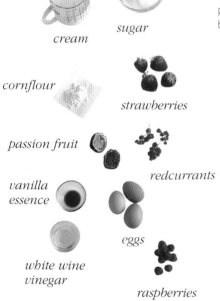

cream

sugar

cornflour

strawberries

passion fruit

redcurrants

*vanilla
essence*

eggs

*white wine
vinegar*

raspberries

Cook's Tip

Draw six 7.5 cm/3 in circles and
pipe smaller meringues, if you
aren't hungry enough for a
monster dessert.

1 Preheat the oven to 140°C/275°F/
Gas 1. In pencil, draw eight 10 cm/4 in
circles on two separate sheets of baking
parchment which will fit on two flat
baking sheets.

2 Put the egg whites into a very
clean, dry bowl and whisk until stiff.
This will take about 2 minutes with an
electric whisk; peaks made in the
meringue should keep their shape
when it's ready. Add the sugar gradually
and whisk well each time. The mixture
should now be very stiff.

3 Use a metal spoon to gently stir in
the cornflour, white wine vinegar and
vanilla essence. Put the meringue into a
large piping bag, fitted with a large
star nozzle.

4 Pipe a solid layer of meringue in four of the drawn circles and then pipe a lattice
pattern in the other four. Put the meringues in the oven and cook for 1¼–1½ hours,
swapping shelf positions after 30 minutes, until lightly browned. The paper will peel
off the back easily when the meringues are cooked.

5 Roughly chop most of the summer
fruits, reserving a few for decoration.
Whip the cream and spread it over the
solid meringue shapes. Scatter the fruit
over. Halve the passion fruit, scoop out
the seeds with a teaspoon and scatter
them over the fruit. Put a lattice lid on
top of each and serve with the
reserved fruits.

Lazy Pastry Pudding

You don't need to be neat to make this pudding as it looks best when it's really craggy and rough. Serve with whipped cream or custard.

Serves 6

INGREDIENTS
225 g/8 oz/2 cups plain flour
15 ml/1 tbsp caster sugar
15 ml/1 tbsp ground mixed spice
150 g/5 oz/⅔ cup butter or margarine
1 egg, separated
450 g/1 lb cooking apples
30 ml/2 tbsp lemon juice
115 g/4 oz/⅔ cup raisins
75 g/3 oz/½ cup demerara sugar
25 g/1 oz/¼ cup hazelnuts, toasted and chopped

lemon   flour   apples

egg

butter   demerara sugar   hazelnuts

caster sugar   raisins

mixed spice

COOK'S TIP
This pudding is delicious served either hot or cold.

1 Put the flour, caster sugar and spice in a bowl and stir. Add the butter or margarine and rub it into the flour with your fingertips, until the mixture looks like breadcrumbs. Add the egg yolk and use your hands to pull the mixture together to make the pastry. (You may need to add a little water.)

2 Turn on to a lightly floured surface and knead gently until smooth. Roll out the pastry to make a rough circle about 30 cm/12 in across. Use the rolling pin to lift the pastry on to a small baking sheet. The pastry should hang over the edges.

3 Peel and slice the apples. Toss them in the lemon juice, to stop them from turning brown. Scatter some of them over the middle of the pastry, leaving a 10 cm/4 in border all round. Reserve 30 ml/2 tbsp of the demerara sugar. Scatter some of the raisins over the top, then some of the remaining demerara sugar. Keep making layers of apple, raisins and sugar until you have used them up.

4 Preheat the oven to 200°C/400°F/Gas 6. Fold up the pastry edges to cover the fruit, overlapping it where necessary. Don't worry too much about neatness. Brush the pastry with the egg white and sprinkle over the reserved demerara sugar. Scatter the nuts over. Cover the central hole with foil, to stop the raisins from burning. Cook for 30–35 minutes, until the pastry is cooked and browned.

Grilled Peaches

A simple, rich dessert that's quick and easy to make. Serve it solo or with cream or yogurt.

Serves 4

INGREDIENTS
115 g/4 oz/1 cup raspberries
30 ml/2 tbsp icing sugar
4 ripe peaches
120 ml/8 tbsp mascarpone
  cheese
45 ml/3 tbsp soft brown sugar

peaches

icing sugar

soft brown sugar

raspberries

mascarpone cheese

1 Reserve a few of the raspberries for decoration and put the rest in a blender with the icing sugar and whizz until smooth. Use a hand-held blender if you prefer, or push the raspberries through a sieve with a wooden spoon and then mix with the sugar.

2 Cut round each peach lengthways and twist the fruit. One half should come away, leaving the stone in the second half. Scoop the stone out and arrange all eight halves on a grill pan, cut-sides up. Preheat the grill.

COOK'S TIP
As the cheese melts, the sugar might slip off, so have some extra handy to sprinkle over the top of the peaches.

3 Put 15 ml/1 tbsp of cheese in the centre of each peach, in the dip left by the stone. Sprinkle the sugar over the top of all the peaches and grill under a medium heat, until the cheese and sugar have melted.

4 Share the raspberry sauce among four plates and arrange the grilled peaches on top. Decorate with the reserved fruit and serve immediately.

Summer Fruit Cheesecake

Making this is much easier than it looks and it tastes so good, it's well worth the effort.

Serves 8–10

INGREDIENTS
175 g/6 oz/¾ cup butter
225 g/8 oz digestive biscuits
rind and juice of 2 lemons
11 g/scant ½ oz sachet gelatine
225 g/8 oz/1 cup cottage cheese
200 g/7 oz/scant 1 cup soft
  cream cheese
400 g/14 oz can condensed milk
450 g/1 lb/4 cups strawberries
115 g/4 oz/1 cup raspberries

condensed milk

butter

lemons

cottage cheese

raspberries

cream cheese

digestive biscuits

strawberries

gelatine

COOK'S TIP
Always add gelatine to the liquid, never the other way round.

1 Cut a piece of greaseproof paper to fit the base of a 20 cm/8 in loose-bottomed springform cake tin. Melt the butter in a saucepan over a low heat. Break the biscuits in pieces, put them in a food processor and whizz until they are crumbs. Stir them into the melted butter until well mixed.

2 Tip the crumbs into the cake tin and use a spoon to spread the mixture in a thin, even layer over the base, pressing down well. Put the tin in the fridge while you make the filling.

3 Put the lemon rind and juice in a small bowl and sprinkle the gelatine over. Stand the bowl in a saucepan of water and heat gently, until the gelatine crystals have all melted. Stir the mixture and leave to cool slightly.

4 Put the cottage cheese in a food processor and whizz for 20 seconds. Add the cream cheese and condensed milk, fix the lid in place again and whizz the mixture. Pour in the dissolved gelatine mixture and whizz once more.

5 Roughly chop half the strawberries and scatter them over the biscuit base. Add half the raspberries, saving the rest for decorating the top. Pour the cheese mixture carefully over the fruit and level the top. Return to the fridge and leave overnight to set.

6 Carefully loosen the edges of the cheesecake with a palette knife. Then stand the cake tin on a large mug or can and gently open the clip at the side of the tin. Allow the tin to slide down. Put the cheesecake on a serving plate and decorate it with the reserved fruit.

Chocolate Cups

Perfect for the chocoholics in the family. Serve
with crisp dessert biscuits.

Serves 4

INGREDIENTS
200 g/7 oz bar plain chocolate
120 ml/4 fl oz/½ cup double
  cream
75 g/3 oz white chocolate

*double
cream*

*white
chocolate*

*plain
chocolate*

1 Break half the plain chocolate into
pieces and put them in a bowl. Stand
the bowl over a pan of hot, but not
boiling, water and leave to melt, stirring
occasionally. Make sure the water
doesn't touch the bowl.

2 Line four ramekins, or similarly sized
cups, with a piece of foil. Don't worry
about it creasing or scrunching up.

3 Use a clean paintbrush to brush the
melted chocolate over the foil in a thick
layer. Chill in the fridge until set. Paint a
second layer and leave to chill again.

4 Put the cream in a bowl and whisk
until stiff. Melt the remaining plain
chocolate as before and use a metal
spoon to fold it into the cream.

5 Roughly chop the white chocolate
and stir it gently into the chocolate and
cream mixture.

6 Carefully peel the foil off the
chocolate cups and fill each one with
the chocolate and cream mixture. Chill
until set.

COOK'S TIP
Try using white chocolate
drops, chocolate-covered raisins
or a chopped chocolate bar,
instead of the white chocolate.

Ice Cream Bombes

This chilly dessert with warm sauce will have you ready to explode – it's dynamite!

Serves 6

INGREDIENTS

1 litre/1¾ pints/4 cups
  soft-scoop chocolate ice cream
475 ml/16 fl oz/2 cups soft-
  scoop vanilla ice cream
50 g/2 oz/⅓ cup plain chocolate
  drops
115 g/4 oz toffees
75 ml/5 tbsp double cream

double cream

vanilla ice cream

chocolate drops

chocolate ice cream

toffees

1 Share the chocolate ice cream between six small cups. Push it roughly to the base and up the sides, leaving a small cup-shaped dip in the middle. Don't worry if it's not very neat; it will be frozen again before the ice cream melts too much. Return to the freezer and leave for 45 minutes. Take it out again and smooth the ice cream into shape. Return to the freezer.

2 Put the vanilla ice cream in a small bowl and break it up slightly with a spoon. Stir in the chocolate drops and then use this mixture to fill the dip in the chocolate ice cream. Return the cups to the freezer and leave overnight.

3 Put the toffees in a small saucepan and heat gently, stirring all the time. As they melt, add the double cream and keep mixing until all the toffees have melted and the sauce is warm.

4 Dip the cups in hot water and run a knife round the edge of the ice cream. Turn out on to individual plates and pour the toffee sauce over the top. Serve immediately.

Puffy Pears

An eye-catching dessert that is simple to make and delicious to eat, especially when served with whipped cream or fromage frais.

Serves 4

INGREDIENTS
225 g/8 oz puff pastry
2 pears, peeled
2 squares plain chocolate,
  roughly chopped
15 ml/1 tbsp lemon juice
1 egg, beaten
15 ml/1 tbsp caster sugar

puff pastry

pears

egg

caster sugar

lemon juice

plain chocolate

1 Roll the pastry into a 25 cm/10 in square on a lightly floured surface. Trim the edges, then cut it into four equal smaller squares.

2 Remove the core from each pear half and pack the gap with the chopped chocolate. Place a pear half, cut-side down, on each piece of pastry and brush them with the lemon juice, to prevent them from going brown.

3 Preheat the oven to 190°C/375°F/ Gas 5. Cut the pastry into a pear shape, by following the lines of the fruit, leaving a 2.5 cm/1 in border. Use the trimmings to make leaves and brush the pastry border with the beaten egg.

4 Arrange the pastry and pears on a baking sheet. Make deep cuts in the pears, taking care not to cut right through the fruit, and sprinkle them with the caster sugar. Cook for 20–25 minutes, until lightly browned. Serve hot or cold.

COOK'S TIP
Try the same thing using eating apples, especially when you have picked the fruit yourself.

Chocolate Brownies

Scout out these delicious, moist and chewy cakes, and guide yourself to a chocolate treat!

Makes 9

INGREDIENTS
65 g/2½ oz/⅓ cup butter
50 g/2 oz plain chocolate
150 g/5 oz/scant 1 cup soft
  brown sugar
2 eggs, beaten
65 g/2½ oz/generous ½ cup
  plain flour
50 g/2 oz/½ cup roughly
  chopped pecans or walnuts
25 g/1 oz/¼ cup icing sugar

icing sugar

soft brown sugar

flour

butter

eggs

plain chocolate

pecans

1 Put the butter and chocolate in a bowl and stand it over a saucepan of hot, but not boiling water. Make sure the water doesn't touch the bowl. Leave until they have both melted and then stir them together.

2 Stir the sugar into the butter and chocolate mixture and leave for a while to cool slightly.

3 Cut a piece of baking parchment or greaseproof paper to fit the base of an 18 cm/7 in square cake tin.

4 Preheat the oven to 180°C/350°F/ Gas 4. Beat the eggs into the chocolate mixture, then stir in the flour and nuts.

5 Pour the mixture into the lined cake tin and level the top. Cook for 25–35 minutes, until firm around the edges but still slightly soft in the middle.

6 Cut into nine squares and leave to cool in the tin. Dredge with a little icing sugar and serve hot or cold.

Bacon Twists

Making bread is always fun, so try this savoury version and add that extra twist to your breakfast. Serve with soft cheese with herbs.

Makes 12

INGREDIENTS
450 g/1 lb/4 cups strong white flour
6 g/¼ oz sachet easy-blend yeast
2.5 ml/½ tsp salt
400 ml/14 fl oz/1¾ cups hand-hot water
12 streaky bacon rashers
1 egg, beaten

water
flour
egg
yeast
salt
bacon

1 Mix the flour, yeast and salt in a bowl and stir them together. Add a little of the water and mix with a knife. Add the remaining water and use your hands to pull the mixture together, to make a sticky dough.

2 Turn the dough on to a lightly floured surface and knead it for 5 minutes, or until the dough is smooth and stretchy.

3 Divide into 12 pieces and roll each one into a sausage shape.

4 Lay each bacon rasher on a chopping board and run the back of the knife down its length, to stretch it slightly. Wind a rasher of bacon round each dough "sausage".

5 Brush the "sausages" with beaten egg and arrange them on a lightly oiled baking sheet. Leave somewhere warm for 30 minutes, or until they have doubled in size. Preheat the oven to 200°C/400°F/Gas 6 and cook the "sausages" for 20–25 minutes, until cooked and browned.

COOK'S TIP
This same basic dough mix can be used to make rolls or a loaf of bread. Tap the base of the breadstick – if it sounds hollow, it's cooked.

Gingerbread Jungle

Snappy biscuits in animal shapes, which can be decorated in your own style.

Makes 14

INGREDIENTS
175 g/6 oz/1½ cups self-raising
  flour
2.5 ml/½ tsp bicarbonate of soda
2.5 ml/½ tsp ground cinnamon
10 ml/2 tsp caster sugar
50 g/2 oz/¼ cup butter
45 ml/3 oz/3 tbsp golden syrup
oil, for baking sheets
50 g/2 oz/½ cup icing sugar
5–10 ml/1–2 tsp water

flour

icing sugar

golden syrup

butter

caster sugar

cinnamon

bicarbonate of soda

1 Preheat the oven to 190°C/375°F/ Gas 5. Put the flour, bicarbonate of soda, cinnamon and caster sugar in a bowl and mix together. Melt the butter and syrup in a saucepan. Pour over the dry ingredients.

2 Mix together well and then use your hands to pull the mixture together to make a dough.

3 Turn onto a lightly floured surface and roll out to a 5 mm/¼ in thickness.

4 Use animal cutters to cut shapes from the dough and arrange them on two lightly oiled baking sheets, leaving enough room between them to rise. Press the trimmings back into a ball, roll it out and cut more shapes. Continue to do this until the dough is used up. Cook for 8–12 minutes, until lightly browned.

5 Leave the biscuits to cool slightly, before lifting them on to a wire rack with a palette knife. Sift the icing sugar into a small bowl and add enough water to make a fairly soft icing. Put the icing in a piping bag fitted with a small, plain nozzle and pipe decorations on the biscuits.

COOK'S TIP

Any cutters can be used with the same mixture. Obviously the smaller the cutters, the more biscuits you will make.

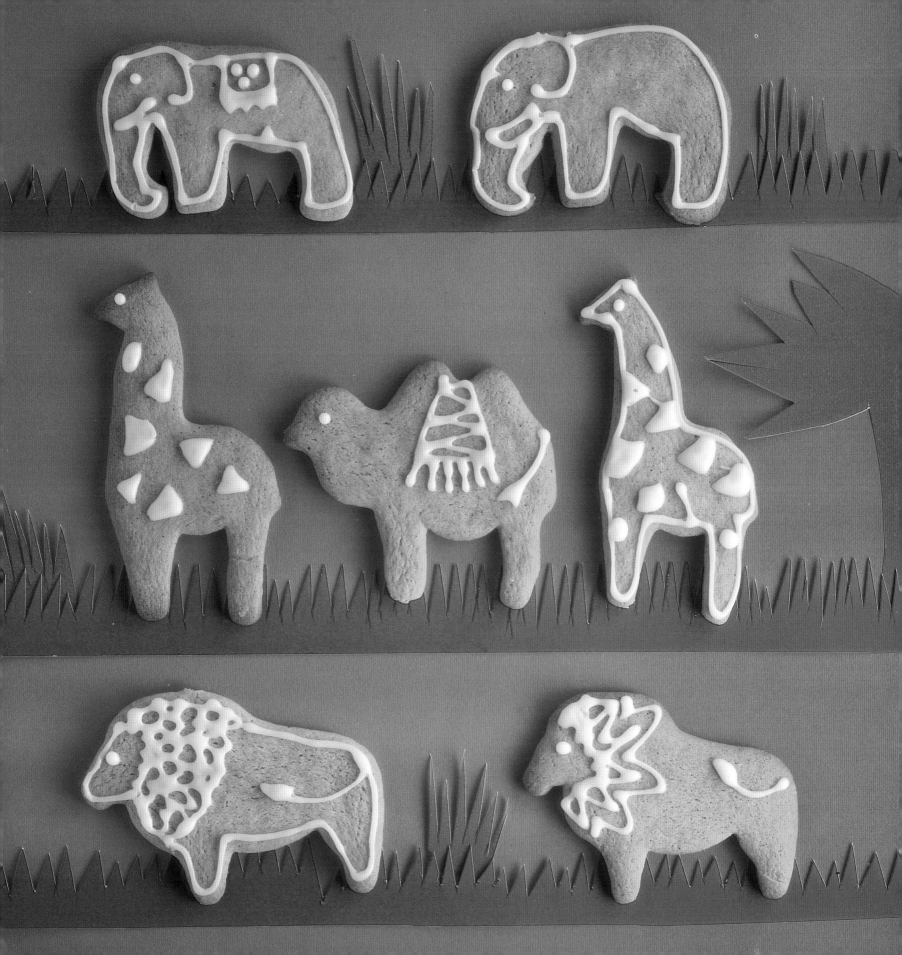

Blueberry Muffins

Monster muffins that contain whole fresh blueberries that burst in the mouth when bitten.

Makes 9

INGREDIENTS
375 g/13 oz/3¼ cups plain flour
200 g/7 oz/scant 1 cup caster
  sugar
25 ml/1½ tbsp baking powder
175 g/6 oz/¾ cup butter,
  roughly chopped
1 egg, beaten
1 egg yolk
150 ml/¼ pint/⅔ cup milk
grated rind of 1 lemon
175 g/6 oz/1½ cups fresh
  blueberries

milk

caster
sugar

flour

baking
powder

egg

egg yolk

lemon

blueberries

butter

1 Preheat the oven to 200°/400°F/ Gas 6. Line a muffin tin with nine large paper muffin cases.

3 In a separate bowl, beat the egg, egg yolk, milk and lemon rind together.

2 Put the flour, sugar, baking powder and butter in a bowl. Use your fingertips to rub the butter into the flour, until the mixture looks like breadcrumbs.

4 Pour the egg and milk mixture into the flour mixture, add the blueberries and mix gently together.

5 Share the mixture among the cake cases and cook for 30–40 minutes, until they are risen and brown.

6 Push a skewer into the middle of one of the muffins. The muffins are cooked if it comes out clean. Lift on to a wire rack to cool.

COOK'S TIP
As the muffins have fresh fruit in them, they will not keep for longer than four days, so best eat them immediately!

Chunky Choc Bars

A no-cook cake that's a smash-hit with everyone.

Makes 12

INGREDIENTS
350 g/12 oz plain chocolate
115 g/4 oz/½ cup butter
400 g/14 oz can condensed milk
225 g/8 oz digestive biscuits,
  broken
50 g/2 oz/⅓ cup raisins
115 g/4 oz ready-to-eat dried
  peaches, roughly chopped
50 g/2 oz hazelnuts or pecans,
  roughly chopped

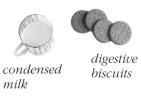

condensed milk

digestive biscuits

hazelnuts

butter

plain chocolate

dried peaches

raisins

1 Line an 18 × 28 cm/7 × 11 in cake tin with clear film.

2 Put the chocolate and butter in a large bowl over a pan of hot but not boiling water (the bowl must not touch the water) and leave to melt. Stir until well mixed.

3 Beat the condensed milk into the chocolate and butter mixture.

4 Add the biscuits, raisins, peaches and nuts and mix well, until all the ingredients are coated in chocolate.

5 Tip the mixture into the prepared tin, making sure it is pressed well into the corners. Leave the top craggy. Put in the fridge and leave to set.

6 Lift the cake out of the tin using the clear film and then peel it off. Cut into 12 bars and keep chilled – until you are ready to eat it!

Peanut Cookies

Packing up a picnic? Got a birthday party coming up? Make sure some of these nutty biscuits are on the menu.

Makes 25

INGREDIENTS
225 g/8 oz/1 cup butter
30 ml/2 tbsp smooth peanut
   butter
115 g/4 oz/1 cup icing sugar
50 g/2 oz/scant ½ cup cornflour
225 g/8 oz/2 cups plain flour
115 g/4 oz/1 cup unsalted
   peanuts

plain flour

cornflour

butter

peanut butter

unsalted-peanuts

icing sugar

1 Put the butter and peanut butter in a bowl and beat together. Add the icing sugar, cornflour and plain flour and mix together with your hands, to make a soft dough.

2 Preheat the oven to 180°C/350°F/ Gas 4 and lightly oil two baking sheets. Roll the mixture into 25 small balls, using floured hands, and place the balls on the two baking sheets. Leave plenty of room for the cookies to spread.

3 Press the tops of the balls of dough flat, using either the back of a fork or your fingertips.

4 Press some of the peanuts into each of the cookies. Cook for 15–20 minutes, until lightly browned. Leave to cool for a few minutes before lifting them carefully on to a wire rack with a palette knife. When they are cool, pack them in a tin.

COOK'S TIP
Make really monster cookies by making bigger balls of dough. Leave plenty of room on the baking sheets for them to spread, though.

Five-Spice Fingers

Light, crumbly biscuits with an unusual Chinese five-spice flavouring.

Makes 28

INGREDIENTS
115 g/4 oz/½ cup margarine
50 g/2 oz/½ cup icing sugar
115 g/4 oz/1 cup plain flour
10 ml/2 tsp five-spice powder
oil, for greasing
grated rind and juice of
½ orange

orange

icing sugar

five-spice powder

margarine

flour

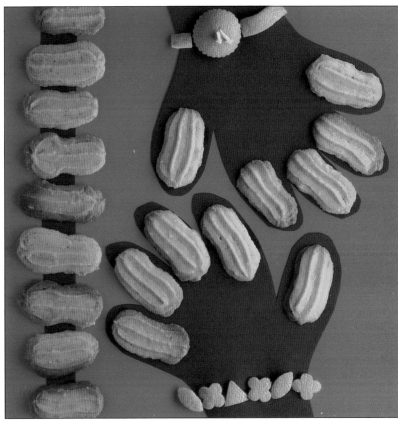

1 Put the margarine and half the icing sugar in a bowl and beat with a wooden spoon, until the mixture is smooth, creamy and soft.

2 Add the flour and five-spice powder and beat again. Put the mixture in a large piping bag fitted with a large star nozzle.

3 Preheat the oven to 180°C/350°F/ Gas 4. Lightly grease two baking sheets and pipe short lines of mixture, about 7.5 cm/3 in long, on them. Leave enough room for them to spread. Cook for 15 minutes, until lightly browned. Leave to cool slightly, before lifting them on to a wire rack with a palette knife.

4 Sift the remaining icing sugar into a small bowl and stir in the orange rind. Add enough juice to make a thin icing and brush it over the biscuits while they are still warm.

COOK'S TIP
Delicious served with ice cream or creamy desserts.

Carrot Cake

This is full of healthy fibre – yet moist and soft at the same time.

Serves 10 –12

INGREDIENTS
225 g/8 oz/2 cups self-raising flour
10 ml/2 tsp baking powder
150 g/5 oz/1 scant cup soft brown sugar
115 g/4 oz ready-to-eat dried figs, roughly chopped
225 g/8 oz carrots, grated
2 small ripe bananas, mashed
2 eggs
150 ml/¼ pint/⅔ cup sunflower oil
175 g/6 oz/¾ cup cream cheese
175 g/6 oz/1½ cups icing sugar, sifted
small coloured sweets, nuts or grated chocolate, to decorate

sunflower oil

dried figs

cream cheese

self-raising flour

baking powder

icing sugar

eggs

carrots

bananas

soft brown sugar

1 Lightly grease an 18 cm/7 in round, loose-based springform cake tin. Cut a piece of baking parchment or grease-proof paper to fit the base of the tin.

2 Preheat the oven to 180°C/350°F/ Gas 4. Put the flour, baking powder and sugar into a large bowl and mix well. Stir in the figs.

3 Using your hands, squeeze as much liquid out of the grated carrots as you can and add them to the bowl. Mix in the mashed bananas.

4 Beat the eggs and oil together and pour them into the mixture. Beat together with a wooden spoon.

5 Spoon into the prepared tin and level the top. Cook for 1–1¼ hours, until a skewer pushed into the centre of the cake comes out clean. Remove the cake from the tin and leave to cool on a wire rack.

6 Beat the cream cheese and icing sugar together, to make a thick icing. Spread it over the top of the cake. Decorate with small coloured sweets, nuts or grated chocolate. Cut in small wedges, to serve.

COOK'S TIP

Because this cake contains moist vegetables and fruit, it will not keep longer than a week, but you probably won't find this a problem!

Lemon Meringue Cakes

This is a variation on fairy cakes – soft lemon sponge topped with crisp meringue.

Makes 18

INGREDIENTS
115 g/4 oz/½ cup margarine
200 g/7 oz/scant 1 cup caster
  sugar
2 eggs
115 g/4 oz/1 cup self-raising
  flour
5 ml/1 tsp baking powder
grated rind of 2 lemons
30 ml/2 tbsp lemon juice
2 egg whites

flour

lemon juice

caster sugar

baking powder *eggs* *lemons*

margarine

2 Beat in the eggs, flour, baking powder, half the lemon rind and all the lemon juice.

3 Stand 18 small paper cases in two bun tins, and share the mixture between them.

1 Preheat the oven to 190°C/375°F/ Gas 5. Put the margarine in a bowl and beat until soft. Add 115 g/4 oz/½ cup of the caster sugar and continue to beat until the mixture is smooth and creamy.

4 Whisk the egg whites in a clean bowl, until they stand in soft peaks.

5 Stir in the remaining caster sugar and lemon rind.

6 Put a spoonful of the meringue mixture on each cake. Cook for 20–25 minutes, until the meringue is crisp and brown. Serve hot or cold.

COOK'S TIP

Make sure that you whisk the egg whites enough before adding the sugar – when you lift out the whisk they should stand in peaks that just flop over slightly at the top.
Use a mixture of oranges and lemons, for a sweeter taste.

Citrus Punch & Spicy Nuts

A knock-out of a cold drink for hot days, served with spicy nuts.

Serves 4

INGREDIENTS
FOR THE CITRUS PUNCH
juice of 2 pink grapefruit
juice of 2 lemons
juice of 4 oranges
150 ml/¼ pint/⅔ cup
   pineapple juice
30 ml/2 tbsp caster sugar
600 ml/1 pint/2½ cups
   lemonade
slices of lime and orange,
   to decorate

FOR THE SPICY NUTS
75 g/3 oz/⅓ cup butter
15 ml/1 tbsp oil
2 garlic cloves, crushed
30 ml/2 tbsp Worcestershire
   sauce
5 ml/1 tsp chilli powder
5 ml/1 tsp ground turmeric
5 ml/1 tsp cayenne pepper
450 g/1 lb/4 cups mixed nuts

pink grapefruit

lemonade

pineapple juice

oranges

lemons

garlic

oil

Worcestershire sauce

turmeric

butter

chilli powder

cayenne pepper

caster sugar

mixed nuts

1 To make the citrus punch, put the fruit juices in a large jug or bowl, stir in the sugar, then chill.

2 Add the lemonade and fruit slices, just before serving.

3 Make the nuts while the punch is chilling. Heat the butter and oil in a frying pan until the butter melts. Stir in the garlic, Worcestershire sauce, spices and seasonings.

4 Cook gently for 1 minute, stirring all the time, then add the nuts and cook for 4–5 minutes, until lightly browned. Drain on kitchen paper and leave to cool before serving with the punch.

Buck's Fizzy & Twizzles

Impress the grown-ups with your own corker of a drink, which will knock spots off the real thing. Serve with savoury cheese twizzles.

Serves 6–8

INGREDIENTS
FOR THE BUCK'S FIZZY
600 ml/1 pint/2½ cups fresh orange juice
45 ml/3 tbsp lemon juice
50 g/2 oz/½ cup icing sugar, sifted
300 ml/½ pint/1¼ cups bitter lemon, chilled
orange slices, to decorate

FOR THE TWIZZLES
225 g/8 oz/2 cups plain flour
115 g/4 oz/½ cup butter, roughly chopped
15 ml/1 tbsp dried mixed herbs
50 g/2 oz mature Cheddar cheese, grated
cold water, to mix
salt and pepper

bitter lemon

flour   *butter*

orange slices   *water*   *cheese*

orange juice   *pepper*

mixed herbs   *icing sugar*

lemon juice

1 To make the Buck's fizzy, mix the orange and lemon juice and the icing sugar in a jug; stir and chill.

2 Just before serving, add the bitter lemon and decorate the jug or the glasses with orange slices.

COOK'S TIP
Make some of the pastry strips into circles. After baking, slip three pastry strips inside each circle so each guest gets his or her personal set of twizzles.

3 Make the twizzles while the Buck's fizzy is chilling. Preheat the oven to 190°C/375°F/Gas 5. Put the flour and the butter in a bowl. Rub in the butter, then stir in the herbs, grated cheese and seasoning and add enough water to be able to pull the pastry together and knead it into a firm dough.

4 Roll out the dough until it is 5 mm/¼ in thick and cut it into 15 cm/6 in strips, about 1 cm/½ in wide. Twist each strip once or twice and arrange them in rows on a greased baking sheet. Cook for 15–20 minutes, until golden brown. Cool the twizzles on a wire rack.

Hot Chocolate & Choc-tipped Biscuits

Get those cold hands wrapped round a steaming hot drink, and tuck into choc-tipped biscuits.

Serves 2

INGREDIENTS
FOR THE HOT CHOCOLATE
90 ml/6 tbsp drinking chocolate powder, plus a little extra for sprinkling
30 ml/2 tbsp sugar, or more according to taste
600 ml/1 pint/2½ cups milk
2 large squirts aerosol cream (optional)

FOR THE CHOC-TIPPED BISCUITS
115 g/4 oz/½ cup soft margarine
45 ml/3 tbsp icing sugar, sifted
150 g/5 oz/1¼ cups plain flour
few drops of vanilla essence
75 g/3 oz plain chocolate

milk

soft margarine

sugar

vanilla essence

drinking chocolate powder

aerosol cream

icing sugar

flour

plain chocolate

1 To make the drinking chocolate, put the drinking chocolate powder and the sugar in a saucepan. Add the milk and bring it to the boil, whisking all the time. Divide between two mugs. Add more sugar if needed. Top with a squirt of cream, if you like.

2 To make the choc-tipped biscuits, put the margarine and icing sugar in a bowl and beat them together until very soft. Mix in the flour and vanilla essence. Preheat the oven to 180°C/350°F/Gas Mark 4 and lightly grease two baking sheets.

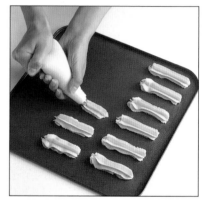

3 Put the mixture in a large piping bag fitted with a large star nozzle and pipe 10–13 cm/4–5 in lines on the baking sheets. Cook for 15–20 minutes, until pale golden brown. Allow to cool slightly before lifting on to a wire rack. Leave the biscuits to cool completely.

4 Put the chocolate in a small bowl. Stand in a pan of hot, but not boiling, water and leave to melt. Dip both ends of each biscuit in the chocolate, put back on the rack and leave to set.

COOK'S TIP
Make round biscuits if you prefer, and dip half of each biscuit in melted chocolate.

Fruit Crush & Fruit Kebabs

Fruit crush is just the ticket on a sultry summer's day, served with mouth-watering fruit kebabs.

Serves 6

INGREDIENTS
FOR THE FRUIT CRUSH
300 ml/½ pint/1¼ cups
  orange juice
300 ml/½ pint/1¼ cups
  pineapple juice
300 ml/½ pint/1¼ cups tropical
  fruit juice
475 ml/16 fl oz/2 cups lemonade
fresh pineapple slices and
  fresh cherries, to decorate

FOR THE FRUIT KEBABS
24 small strawberries
24 green seedless grapes
12 marshmallows
1 kiwi fruit, peeled and cut in
  12 wedges
1 banana
15 ml/1 tbsp lemon juice

tropical fruit juice   *pineapple juice*   *orange juice*

lemonade   *pineapple slices*   *kiwi fruit*

banana

 grapes   *lemon juice*

marshmallows

strawberries   *cherries*

1 To make the fruit crush, put the orange juice and the pineapple juice into ice-cube trays and freeze them until solid.

2 Mix together the tropical fruit juice and lemonade in a large jug. Put a mixture of the ice cubes in each glass and pour the fruit crush over. Decorate the glasses with the pineapple slices and cherries.

3 To make the fruit kebabs, thread 2 strawberries, 2 grapes, a marshmallow and a wedge of kiwi fruit on to each of twelve wooden skewers.

4 Peel the banana and cut it into twelve slices. Toss it in the lemon juice and thread on to the skewers. Serve immediately.

Strawberry Smoothie & Stars-in-your-Eyes Biscuits

A real smoothie that's lip-smackingly special, when served with crunchy stars-in-your-eyes biscuits.

Serves 4–6

INGREDIENTS

FOR THE STRAWBERRY SMOOTHIE
225 g/8 oz/2 cups strawberries
150 ml/¼ pint/⅔ cup Greek
  yogurt
475ml/16fl oz/2 cups ice-cold
  milk
30 ml/2 tbsp icing sugar

FOR STARS-IN-YOUR-EYES BISCUITS
115 g/4 oz/½ cup butter
175 g/6 oz/1½ cups plain flour
50 g/2 oz/¼ cup caster sugar
30 ml/2 tbsp golden syrup
30 ml/2 tbsp preserving sugar

milk

flour

Greek yogurt

icing sugar

golden syrup

strawberries

preserving sugar

caster sugar

butter

1 First make the stars-in-your-eyes biscuits: put the butter, flour and sugar in a bowl and rub in the fat with your fingertips, until the mixture looks like breadcrumbs. Stir in the caster sugar and then knead together to make a ball. Chill in the fridge for 30 minutes.

2 Preheat the oven to 180°C/350°F/ Gas 4 and lightly grease two baking sheets. Roll out the dough on a floured surface to a 5 mm/¼ in thickness and use a 7.5 cm/3 in star-shaped cutter to stamp out the biscuits.

3 Arrange the biscuits on a baking sheet, leaving enough room for them to rise. Press the trimmings together and keep rolling out and cutting more biscuits until all the mixture has been used. Bake for 10–15 minutes, until they are golden brown.

4 Put the syrup in a small microwave-safe bowl and heat it on HIGH for 12 seconds or heat for 1-2 minutes over simmering water. Brush over the biscuits while they are still warm. Sprinkle a little preserving sugar on top of each one and leave to cool.

5 To make the strawberry smoothies, reserve a few of the strawberries for decoration and put the rest in a blender with the yogurt. Whizz until fairly smooth.

6 Add the milk and icing sugar, process again and pour into glasses. Serve each glass decorated with one or two of the reserved strawberries.

INDEX